DO YOU HEAR ME, HONEY?

Y0-BZK-762

DO YOU HEAR ME, HONEY?

The Distortions of Family Communication

John W. Drakeford

HARPER & ROW, PUBLISHERS

NEW YORK

EVANSTON

SAN FRANCISCO

LONDON

DO YOU HEAR ME, HONEY? Copyright © 1976 by John W. Drakeford. All rights reserved. Printed in the United States of America. No part of this book may be used or reproduced in any manner whatsoever without written permission except in the case of brief quotations embodied in critical articles and reviews. For information address Harper & Row, Publishers, Inc., 10 East 53rd Street, New York, N.Y. 10022. Published simultaneously in Canada by Fitzhenry & Whiteside Limited, Toronto.

FIRST EDITION

Designed by C. Linda Dingler.

Library of Congress Cataloging in Publication Data
Drakeford, John W
  Do you hear me, honey?
  Includes bibliographical references.
  1. Family.   2. Interpersonal communication.
I. Title.
HQ734.D796 1976   301.42'7   75-12287
ISBN 0-06-062061-7

76 77 78 79 10 9 8 7 6 5 4 3 2 1

to
RON ROBERTSON

a fair dinkum Aussie, friend,
encourager, and magnificent
communicator

Contents

Preface   ix

Introduction   1

The Hazards of the Birth of a Message

1. In the Beginning—a Thought   13
2. Suiting Up Your Thoughts   24
3. The Way You Say It Makes the Difference   39
4. Your Actions Speak So Loudly . . .   50

Trouble on the Channel

5. Why Honey Doesn't Hear   67
6. Talking Down and Talking Up   82
7. Uses and Abuses of Silence   97
8. Low Booster Power   107

Roger—Message Received, or Was It?

9. Getting the Message   119
10. Strange Things People Hear   126
11. The Emotional Short Circuit   134
12. Taming the One-eyed Monster   145
13. You Heard, But Did You Listen?   155
14. The Other Dimension   166

Epilogue   173

Notes   175

Preface

Communication has been a major interest in my life. As an adolescent, I sat listening to a man. With very little formal education, he had a remarkable native fluency, and as he spoke —preaching in a church—I wondered at his persuasive ability. My imagination took flight. "Could I possibly speak like that?" I tried—using his material, without permission—and found a ready acceptance.

At first it was speaking—in churches and anywhere I could find a group of willing listeners—then lecturing, recording, television, narrating a movie, and teaching. Along with my communication interests I followed my life work in psychology and counseling. A combination of these two interests led me to conducting conferences on home and family life.

Inevitably I turned to writing and discovered the difference between oral and written communication. I soon realized the truth of Winston Churchill's statement, "Writing a book was an adventure. To begin with it was a toy, an amusement; then it became a mistress, and then a master, and then a tyrant." Under the sway of that tyrant I found such fulfillment that I wanted to join with the Hebrew slave who, offered his freedom, responded, "I love my master, I will not go free."

The idea for a book on communication had frequently crossed my mind, and at last I decided to put it down on paper. Years of experience in a counseling center led me to conclude any type of family difficulty could be solved if the subjects learned really to communicate with each other. The *if* was the problem.

One of the most remarkable examples of communication through the printed page came from the pen of Elmer Hubbard. His writing, which he himself described as "a literary trifle," a "preachment," in pamphlet form, rolled from the presses until some forty million copies of his *A Message to Garcia* made it one of the most widely read pieces of literature ever produced. It has the theme of responsibility in communication.

When President McKinley needed to send a message to Garcia, the leader of the rebel insurgents in Cuba, he faced insuperable problems—no mails, telegraphs, or other means of communication. Then came the suggestion, "There is a fellow by the name of Rowan, and he will find Garcia if anyone can."

The president sent for Rowan, handed over the message, and said, "Deliver this to Garcia."

Rowan wrapped the letter in an oilskin pouch and disappeared into the night. Four days later he landed on the coast of Cuba, plunged into the jungle, and within three weeks reappeared on the other side of the island having delivered the precious message.

Hubbard had found a man indeed—a man with initiative.

This gave Hubbard the idea for his "literary trifle." Expounding his point, Hubbard suggested a scenario for the modern-day version of *A Message to Garcia*.

An employer calls a clerk into his office and says, "Write me a memo on Correggio." Will the clerk quietly say, "Yes, sir," and go and do the task? No he will look at you with fishy eyes and ask: "Who was he? Which encyclopedia? Where is the encyclopedia? Was I hired for that?"

"Then," said Hubbard, "he'll go off and enlist some other clerks to help him, and there's a good chance he'll return and say, 'Sorry, there's no such man.' By this time the jaded boss will probably respond, 'Never mind, I'll look for it myself.' "

Hubbard contrasted this commonplace present-day attitude with that of Rowan and presented the diligent officer as an example of the "man whose form should be cast in deathless bronze and the statue placed on every college in the land."

The message of Rowan is the message of responsibility in communication. It is the willingness to commit oneself, use some initiative, launch into the adventure of communication.

I hope the readers of this volume will be as willing as Rowan to do something about communicating. If they do, untold possibilities lie ahead.

JOHN W. DRAKEFORD

DO YOU HEAR ME, HONEY?

Introduction

The Delicate Condition of Family Communication

"Hi, honey." Harvey Horton kisses his wife, Dolly, on the cheek and hangs his coat in the closet with the satisfaction that comes to a man having completed a good day's work and now home for the evening hour.

Dropping into his easy chair, Horton opens the paper, buries his head within its pages, and from his paper tent obliquely addresses his spouse, "Did you have a good day?"

"I guess so."

"Play tennis?"

"No."

"What did you do?"

"Nothing."

"Is something wrong?"

"No."

"Sure?"

With vehemence, "*Of course, I'm sure.*"

If Harvey accepts Dolly's statement at face value and says no more, there's a distinct possibility she will later chide him with, "You were so interested in that stupid paper you didn't even notice I was upset."

Jim Hayman is sitting at the cafeteria table with a few buddies from work. The subject is wives, and Hayman has the floor: "My wife, Gracie, is the most versatile woman I know. She makes her own clothes, looks after the kids, keeps house remarkably well, and is an unusually good cook. Why, the food they serve here is only crud compared with the meals Gracie prepares. She's an amazing gal—sure is."

But that night at home, after an awkward discussion about the clothing bill that has just arrived, Gracie puts down liver and onions before him, and he blows his stack. As the retorts grow warmer, he declares, "You're a sorry cook. You couldn't even get a job in a hamburger joint!"

Gloria Harrison has been in a session with her friend Nancy Jefferson, telling about the way Jim committed them for payments on a new automobile when she really wanted a mink coat. She brings her tirade to a conclusion by declaring, "I hate my husband."

What's going on here?
—Dolly Horton tells her husband there's nothing wrong, but her attitude says, "Everything's messed up."
—Jim Hayman complains to his wife about her cooking, but to the men whose opinion he prizes, he remarks that she is a great cook.
—Gloria Harrison, who loves her husband deeply, indicates the fact by the fervor with which she declares, "I hate him."
We're in a topsy-turvy world of communications between husband and wife. Isn't it ridiculous the way husbands and wives experience difficulties relating to each other? It certainly shows that the institution of marriage is not what it's cracked up to be, and it might well be that we'll have to rethink the whole thing.
Well, yes and no.
I once took an organized overseas tour which provided, not only a contact with other cultures, but also a fascinating study of the effects of close living on interpersonal relationships.
Two middle-aged sisters, reared in a fine large family, had been very close to each other across the years. In many ways the tour was for them a return to the days of their girlhood. But after three weeks of traveling on a bus and sharing a room, they had a difference of opinion which left their relationship in a state of disrepair for the remainder of the trip.
A couple of men, bachelor and widower, business associates

for a long period, had eagerly anticipated their experiences as roommates on the tour. Two weeks out, after one hectic and tiring day they went to their motel room to become embroiled in a violent disagreement over who was going to sleep in the bed with the reading lamp. Following this altercation, they maintained a resolute posture of silence toward each other and caused the whole tour group to align themselves as either the Harry or Ken backers, there being no neutral ground.

As a psychologist I speculated about the immaturity of these adults and what I could do to bring some rationality into the situation. Then one day we were eating in a crowded Dutch hotel.

Baldheaded Mr. Harrison had managed to gain possession of the solitary salt shaker and instead of handing it over in response to my plea, passed it to his own little clique. As I sat there eating my insipid food, I darkly speculated as to what miserable plot he was involved in against me and how easy it would be to organize a block of fellow tourists against him.

If some well-educated people could not adjust very well for a close-living, thirty-day period, it is something of a feat that many couples live together day in and day out for long periods of years with not too many serious differences.

Many of these problems of husband-wife living arise from the inherent nature of human beings. Of man, Aristotle said he is "a political animal," Seneca, "a social animal," Shakespeare, "a poor bare forked animal," Mark Twain, "the only animal that blushes or needs to," Maslow, "a perpetually wanting animal." Alongside these evaluations we may need to place another: "Man is a perpetually *communicating* being," and this constant, continuing communicating activity of human beings brings with it a multiplicity of problems.

You Cannot *Not* Communicate

Mr. Halifax is filling out the information form at the counseling center. He has reached the place where the form says, "List the problems in order of importance to you." Mr. Halifax ponders his situation for some time and then takes pen in hand and writes, "My wife and I don't communicate with each other."

Of course, Mr. Halifax was wrong. The Halifaxes were experiencing communication problems, but it wasn't a matter of "not communicating." True, they mightn't be verbalizing anything; talking and communicating are not the same. They were probably going their several ways with no greeting, responses, or conversations; but they were communicating—strange, hostile, defiant, mixed-up messages.

Our basic premise in considering family communication will be: *"You cannot not communicate."*

The family communication system begins with a man and a woman. In dating days they each focus attention on the other, and communication takes place in long conversations, periods spent gazing at each other, and bodily contact of various types. After marriage they settle down and begin to take each other for granted. Then children arrive.

Children bring an extra to family life and provide for a whole group of new relationships, enriching the family experience, but—here's the catch—these little angels can also bring with them a whole raft of devilish potentialities for complicating and disrupting family communications as is seen in a brief incident in the life of Joe Smith.

Joe Smith set up his slide projector in the living room. Mrs. Smith, John, aged fourteen, Tim, ten, and Nancy, six years old, have positioned themselves at vantage points across the room. Lights off—Joe flashes a picture of a map of Canada and begins to tell the story of his recent fishing and hunting expedition. Joe is communicating a message to his family.

How can we analyze the process? One way of describing communication is to say it involves a speaker, a message, and an audience. This idea has proved useful, but it oversimplified the process and depicted a speaker passing on his message to a docile, receptive audience.

Not so Joe Smith's audience. A few minutes into the show, Mrs. Smith interrupted, "But how did you cook food in the canoe?" Nancy, who had to go to the bathroom, tripped over the extension cord and plunged the projector room into blackness. A little later John received a call on the phone and spoke so loudly that his father couldn't concentrate on his narration. Just at the moment when Joe had shown his prize picture of a giant grizzly, Tim fell off the chair, letting out a loud cry of dismay, turning the slide show into a rescue operation. No sooner under way again than Nancy, returning from her excursion, demanded, "Please go back to the slide of the big fish." John declared himself against a rerun and urged Nancy to hush. His sister burst into tears, and the whole family chose sides in the debate of John versus Nancy.

Message-signals bounced around the Smith household with the velocity and variety of directions of the ball at an exhibition of the Harlem Globetrotters.

Even if there were no patterns of interaction and the communication went from one member of the family to another, it's still a complex procedure.

Communication Is a Chain of Events

Communication is a chain of events—a step-by-step process—and understanding the steps gives us some clues as to where family communication goes astray.

The case of Brad White provides a starting point.

Brad White is communicating with his father, telling his parent he feels his allowance should be raised. He commences with an *information source*, recalling the reports of his friends about their allowances. He has decided that his financial remuneration is inequitable and has concluded that he should do some negotiating about the situation. Brad proceeds to *encode* his message. Trying to be tactful, he takes great care in choosing the words he uses to address his father. His father frequently complains that Brad mumbles; so Brad *transmits* his message by enunciating his words as clearly as he can. The message moves along the *channel*, traveling from Brad's mouth to Mr. White's ears. Mr. White is the *receiver*, and he looks straight at Brad so he can both see and hear him in order to get Brad's message.

The elder White is busily engaged in *decoding*—trying to

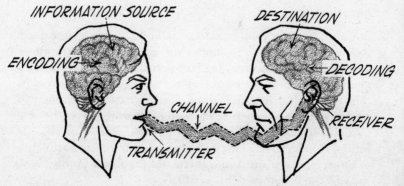

The chain of events in Brad White's communication with his father

make sure he understands what Brad means when he sprinkles his message with such words as *bread, cat,* and *pad.* The message arrives at its *destination*—Mr. White evaluates the proposition and weighs the pros and cons of increasing his offspring's allowance.

Though this may sound fairly simple, it is actually an over-simplification of an infinitely complex operation which, like all complicated procedures, can easily get out of gear. The main problem comes from the nature of the communication experience. Because it is a chain of events, communication is vulnerable as each of these events comes to pass. Beginning in one family member's brain and following in sequence until the destination of another family member's brain is reached, the process can easily be disrupted at a number of sensitive spots which we will call *distortion points.* Because a chain is only as strong as its weakest link, each of these points is of the greatest significance.

Seven distortion points can be seen in the Brad White incident. As Brad thinks about his situation, he may have some wrong ideas—Type A Distortion. When he puts his thoughts into words, he may make the wrong choice—Type B Distortion. As he speaks his words, he could make an emphasis that would change the meaning—Type C Distortion. A plane flying overhead may interfere with the message as it is passing to Mr. White's ears—Type D Distortion. Mr. White's hearing may not be the best and may give rise to a Type E Distortion.

Puzzling over his offspring's language, Mr. White may experience a Type F Distortion, and as he considers the proposition, a Type G Distortion may complicate the message.

This brief description illustrates the complexity of family communication. To say merely that a family has a communication problem is a gross oversimplification.

The year 1974 brought to light an extortion plot of gargantuan proportions. Electric power for the state of Oregon is carried over a network of lines supported by transmission towers reaching upwards of seventy feet into the sky. In a short period of time, thirteen of these towers, located in the vicinity of the city of Portland, were dynamited. An extortion note delivered to the authorities threatened continued destruction of towers unless they paid one million dollars in ransom money.

Because of the impossibility of knowing where the extortionist might strike next among the six thousand transmission towers within a fifty mile radius of Oregon, the whole state became vulnerable.

Family life has a number of vulnerable spots where communication can be disrupted. Like the embattled power authority, our families can be aware of the generalized threat but uncertain as to how to go about finding and managing the trouble spots. In future chapters we will pinpoint seven possible distortion points in family communication and seek to lay plans for counteracting the potential disruption.

A Plan for Developing Communication Skills

If all that's been said about family communication so far is true and if communication is a learned skill, it's time to take action. Here's your plan for building communication skills.

(1) *Grasp the concept of distortion points*. There's a lot of material available on the theory of communication; read as much as you can. Notice particularly the diagram on page 10, explaining the idea of distortion points. Note the way in which distortions enter at seven points to confuse our communication. This outline will give you an overview of communication

problems and make the study of the various chapters dealing with these distortion points of greater value to you.

(2) *Develop the ability to analyze the communication patterns within your own family group.* As you listen, note who communicated well and who communicated poorly. Ask yourself: Why did it happen? Why was that particular communication successful? Why was that communication a failure? Note the strengths of a good communication effort and the weaknesses of a poor communication attempt.

(3) *Study your own communication behavior.* This will probably be the most difficult task of all. Haney[1] reports surveying hundreds of people in organizations and asking them how they evaluated their personal communication skills. Almost all his respondents felt they were doing at least as well as, and in most cases better than, other members of their organization. The results of this test indicate that people are not really aware of their own communication difficulties. Start out with a humble spirit. As you interact with your spouse and children, keep a close tab on what is going on. Note the way you misunderstand people or they misunderstand you.

(4) *Undertake a program of improving your communication skills.* In the materials that follow, take each of the distortion points and see if you are guilty of these types of miscommunication. Rehearse what your are going to say to someone. Speak it into a tape recorder. Play it back. Honestly now, if someone else had made that statement to you, would you have understood it? After you get through a bad communication experience, ask yourself, "What could I have done to improve that?" Study the "Over to You" sections which follow each chapter and put these ideas into practice.

(5) *Use your family as a communication laboratory.* Teach your children communication skills. Follow the plans that have been particularly devised for use with your family
—as you sit to eat your meal
—while talking with your children
—by the way in which you refuse a request
—in the process of physical contact (touching, hugging)
—by learning to listen and by demonstrating listening skills

—while you negotiate with your teenager

—as you learn to offer criticism to family members

—as you develop feedback skills

—in the course of the special games that you play with your children.

OVER ⟶ TO ⟶ YOU

I once visited a ham radio operator who attempted to contact a friend of mine in Australia. After a period of flipping switches, twiddling dials and knobs, and making sundry adjustment, we finally made contact.

Across the thousands of miles my friend's voice came in loud and clear. He concluded his opening statements with, "Over to you." I went ahead with greetings and chatter and in turn gave him an "Over to you."

This book emphasizes both the giving and the receiving aspects of communication. To make this two-way experience practical, many chapters will end with an "Over to You" section.

Here is your chance. Make the most of your opportunity to respond. In some instances "Over to You" will call for you to consider certain salient ideas. In other chapters there are specific responses for you to make.

Try your first "Over to You" on the following page. Consider this somewhat more technical presentation of the basic theory of distortion points. Each distortion point will be discussed in a successive chapter of the book. Don't be frightened by the chart. It is really quite simple, but if you have difficulty in understanding it, don't spend too much time puzzling over it. You can come back later.

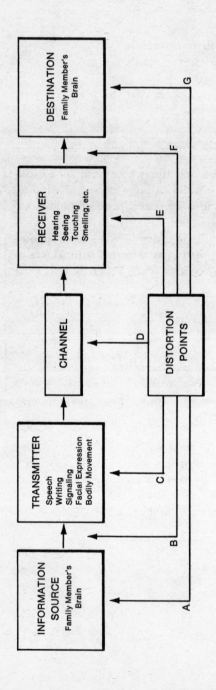

The seven distortion points in family communication are: At the information source, the brain of a member of the family (TYPE A); in the translation of the message from the brain as it is prepared for the mouth or other transmitting organ (TYPE B); during the expression of the message by speech (TYPE C1) or nonverbally (TYPE C2); as the message passes on the air channel between members of the group —moving horizontally (TYPE D1) or vertically (TYPE D2), affected by silence (TYPE D3) or lacking a booster (TYPE D4); when the message is received by a family member's receptor organs, ears, eyes, etc. (TYPE E); as the message is decoded (TYPE F1) or triggers emotional reactions in one or more of the group (TYPE F2); and when it reaches the brain of one or more of the family members and is uncritically accepted (TYPE G1) or not comprehended (TYPE G2).

The Hazards of the Birth
of a Message

A message may die in its birth as an individual struggles to formulate his ideas, translate them into words or actions, and express them.

1. In The Beginning—a Thought

Type A Distortions: Confused Thinking about Family Life

A child comes into the world communicating with a cry, the most thrilling sound ever heard by the human ear. The cry of the newborn says, "Here I am, world, I've arrived. Make way for me, but above everything else fill me in on what happened before I got here."

Some task this. Some scientists claim we've accumulated more scientific knowledge in the last five years than in all previous history, and the storehouse of this world's knowledge continues to fill at an amazing speed. To grasp this, the newly arrived child will have to develop unusual communication skills.

Helen Keller demonstrates the process. Born a normal child, nineteen months later overtaken by a mysterious illness, she lingered at death's door. Then suddenly and unaccountably she recovered. To her parents' dismay, however, the illness had left Helen deaf and blind; and because of her deafness, she was mute.

Helen became, in her own words, ". . . a Phantom living in a world that was no-world."[1] She describes herself as "wild, unruly, giggling and chuckling to express pleasure; kicking, scratching, uttering the choked screams of the deaf mute to indicate the opposite." She was condemned to stay in this "no-world" for five years.

Then the dedicated teacher, Anne Sullivan, began to work with Helen. At first there was little response. Helen explains,

"Alas, the Phantom had no sense of 'natural' bonds with humanity."[2]

After a frustrating month, and on the day earlier marked by a ferocious outburst of temper, there finally came the moment of breakthrough. Down at the well, redolent with the smell of honeysuckle, the ever-diligent teacher placed one of the little blind girl's hands under the flowing, icy cold water. All the while she ceaselessly spelt out the word *water* into Helen's other hand. Then for Helen, in her own words, ". . . somehow the mystery of language was revealed to me. I knew then that 'w-a-t-e-r' meant the wonderful cool something that was flowing over my hand."[3]

She said, "That living word awakened my soul, gave it light, hope, joy, set it free."[4]

Words now had significance. Previously Helen had struggled to learn a meaningless series of letters; now they combined into words representing something. She learned many words that day, just how many she could never recollect, but she recalled, "I do know that mother, father, sister, teacher, were among them—words that were to make the world blossom for me 'like Aaron's rod with flowers.' "

These words made "the world blossom" because they were terms of relationship. Because Helen had no comprehension of experiences of relationship up to this time, it is easy to understand why she had lived in "no-world."

Harry Stack Sullivan says that personality is "the relatively enduring pattern of recurrent interpersonal situations which characterize a human life." If people are going to realize their potential, they must relate to other individuals.

When an individual finds some way to communicate, it helps him to break out of his skin-enclosed isolation and establish word linkages with the world around him and to enter the community of experience. Without someone to give her information, Helen would have remained in "no-world." As a series of people communicated with her, first her teacher, then the family, Helen avidly sought to know the world around her. The imprisoned splendor escaped, and Helen became one of the great creative personalities of her day.

Back to our newly arrived baby. What sort of information will he or she receive?

Ruth, the servant girl in Gilbert and Sullivan's comic opera *Pirates of Penzance,* made a simple mistake. Told to apprentice the boy Frederick to a pilot, Ruth misunderstood the instruction and indentured him to learn the trade of a pirate. Slight difference! From the time he was five years old, Ruth sheltered Frederick from all female company and led him to believe she was the prettiest girl in the world. When he was twenty-two years of age, Frederick met a bevy of beautiful girls. This experience proved quite a revelation, and he turned on Ruth accusing her of deceiving him.

As an individual develops his store of knowledge, he depends upon people to supply him with information—family, friends, teachers, the community in which he lives. Unfortunately, these may not always give him a true and realistic picture of the world in which he will spend the rest of his days.

Wanda Harrison is dabbing her face in a studied effort to save something of the make-up she had applied earlier in the day. Her husband is gently holding her in his arms in much the same manner as a father trying to comfort a distraught child.

This was their first big fuss in twelve months of marriage. Now they are in a process of making-up, and both feel a little foolish about the experience, inwardly resolving it will never happen again.

Between sniffles and dabbing, Wanda speaks, "It was my fault. I always thought husbands liked to bring their wives coffee in bed."

"I always thought."

Probably no experience in life is entered upon with such high expectations as is marriage, and husband and wife generally believe remarkable things are going to happen to them in this relationship. Their ideas have come from a number of sources—friends, parents, relatives, TV, novels—and many of these are bound to be false.

"I always thought" reaches into all areas of family life.

"Wives like to get up early and prepare a good breakfast."

"My husband would never as much as make a sideways glance at another woman."

"Marriage should be like a perpetual honeymoon."

In these expressions we confront an axiom of communication: *There is a difference between fact and opinion.* The essence of our problem lies in what has been called an individual's "conscious or unconscious false assumptions." Many ideas accepted across the years are not necessarily correct. We may sincerely hold them, but sincerity is no guarantee of veracity. As the nineteenth-century humorist Artemus Ward put it, "It ain't the things we don't know that hurt us. It's the things we know that ain't so."

The "I always thought" premise is one of these glittering generalities called by communications writer Haney the "allness" idea. The premise is called into play when the individual (1) is convinced it is possible to know everything about any subject, (2) thinks what he is saying is all that needs to be said on the subject.

Most of us feel more comfortable when we are dealing with certainties. A piece of doggerel states it:

> Just when the speaker convinces me
> Of what he has brillantly planned
> Just when I bow to his wisdom he says
> 'On the other hand . . .'

But this yearning for certainty may cause us to overlook some of the very important considerations. On one occasion Patrick Moynihan said, "One of our greatest weaknesses as Americans is the habit of reducing the most complex issues to the most simplistic moralisms."

To tackle this variety of Type A Distortions we must:

(1) Develop a certain humility. A little ditty puts it like this:

> All things I thought I knew but now confess
> The more I know I know I know I know the less.

We must always remain open to the possibility of new information on the subject.

(2) Learn to differentiate as well as generalize. We have de-

veloped a much greater tendency to notice the way things are alike rather than the way in which they differ. Look for differences.

(3) Try a *which* pinpoint.

"Wives always get up to fix breakfast for their husbands."

> *Which* wives?
>
> *Which* husbands?

"A husband would never even glance sideways at another woman."

> *Which* husband?
>
> *Which* woman?

The computer people have given us a word *Gigo*, which being interpreted is "Garbage in garbage out." This doesn't only apply to computers. The communication experience begins with an information source. If the original information or presuppositions are messed up, there will be Type A Distortion.

The confused thinking may even become serious enough to qualify as a mental illness, for the information source is the human brain. This delicate control center can get out of gear with disastrous results, often referred to as "mental illness," "insanity," or even "madness."

Rougemont, the Swiss philosopher, has said that marriage killed romance because romance was so unreal with the lover forever reaching toward his beloved who kept constantly evading his grasp. But the moment of marriage dispelled this notion by bringing certainty.

While there are reasons for rejecting this thesis, no one can doubt that romantic love in its extreme forms has many pathological aspects. Even the ancient Greeks recognized this and referred to love as a type of madness.

Love may be conveniently divided into three levels: *eros*, *philia*, and *agape*. *Eros* is the sexual, emotional, romantic aspect of love; *phila*, the rational, companionate, intellectual element; and *agape*, the giving or volitional level. In any family experience of love these three elements are present, but during the early dating days which are surrounded by the aura of romance, the *eros* element predominates.

If romantic love is a prelude to marriage and if communication is basic to a good marriage relationship, dating days should be spent in developing verbal communication. But this seldom happens. Kids caught up in romantic love generally move on to secondary sexual experiences, necking, petting, and heavy petting. In these experiences they seldom communicate verbally. Very infrequently do they stop and ask, "Where is this leadings us? What will be the end of it?"

The experiences of these days generally bring conscious or unconscious guilt that dampens discussion just at the time when it is needed most. This irrational emphasis on romantic love leads a couple to spend little time in any type of serious discussion and may mean that a man and a woman enter into the intimate marriage relationship with few of the skills necessary for adequate communication.

Another possible source of Type A Distortions lies in the unwillingness of family members to stretch their intellectual muscles by clarifying their thought processes, and distortions in communication may come from fuzzy thinking.

Administration experts say the first step in all communication is for the would-be communicator to crystallize his own thinking so he has a good, logical grasp of his concepts before he tries to pass them on to others—listeners become confused because the speaker himself was confused in formulating his ideas. A good leader is a clear thinker rather than a profound thinker. Rather unfortunately, the thinking of many would-be communicators is neither profound nor clear.

The same situation prevails within many family units when an unpremeditated statement is hurled out to confuse the recipients. Writing an answer to a serviceman's question, a columnist stated, "Your mouth seems to go on active duty while your brain is on furlough." Many family members are prone to the same type of thoughtless loquacity.

Another variation of Type A Distortions is that type of message-signal referred to by communication theorists as *intrapersonal feedback*, an experience in which a family member makes a statement for the purpose of clarifying his thinking, but this mixed-up thought is received and taken at face value by other family members.

One of the capacities distinguishing man from other forms of animal life is his ability to imagine and anticipate the outcome of his experiences. Apparently cats and dogs don't sit down and speculate as to what it might be like if they were lions and tigers, but man can mentally rehearse and envisage all sorts of possibilities.

At its best this capacity means a human can conceive possibilities of the future and in his imaginings plan an entirely new type of experience that will be beneficial both to him and to his fellows. This we may call vision.

At its worst this ability means an individual, unhappy with life, can withdraw into an imaginary fantasy world, completely divorced from reality. Such a one was Thurber's character, Walter Mitty, a poor milquetoast of a man completely dominated by his wife and mother-in-law. Periodically lapsing into fantasy, he saw himself as a great surgeon, a broncobuster, a sea captain, or some other heroic figure, rather than the poor, henpecked person he was in actual fact. The Mitty-type person spends his days in fantasy, and life passes him by.

How can a human tell whether his ideas are actually rooted in reality or are mere ephemeral fantasy? One clue to this problem lies in the *test of verbalization*. Using this test an individual no longer continues to mull over the matter in his mind. He exteriorizes it. He places it out in the open and takes a fresh look at it. Most of us can only formulate an idea clearly when we put it into words.

An individual probably does this best when he applies the test of verbalization by seeking to convey his idea to another person. As he exteriorizes the idea by relating it to someone else, observing the way another responds to it, he is able to reevaluate the concept and sometimes sees its complete irrationality.

Counselors have long been aware of this phenomenon. A distraught counselee comes in, pours out his story, verbalizing the strange interpretation which he has long turned over in his mind. Frequently, even at the moment of expression, he will begin to correct himself, "No, that's not right—it couldn't really be that way. It's just that I've been thinking so much about it I've lost my sense of proportion."

Verbally expressing thoughts often provides a corrective which enables people to see things in their true perspective. The process is not inevitable, but its possibility is a reason people need someone who, rather than passing judgment, will be willing to listen sympathetically.

At a large gathering of psychiatrists and ministers, one of the psychiatrists addressed himself to the rhetorical question of why these busy people had taken time to attend this conference. He referred to his own hopes for this experience: "How can I know what I think until I hear myself say it?"

A communication can easily be distorted at the information point, and we must allow for Type A Distortions in family life. A member of a family makes statements that sound strange and mixed-up, which in fact they are, and for this reason he desperately needs to exteriorize his thoughts by verbalizing them. As he expresses himself, he may change his point of view. What sometimes sounds like an effort at family communication may actually be an attempt to clarify one member's thoughts. If this person is to be helped, the rest of the family must learn to suspend judgment and allow him to verbalize without holding him responsible for every statement he utters.

One genre of Type A Distortions is profitable. The writer who can deceive in his presentation and give his reader a series of false leads that will divert him from the true facts is the most successful in his field. This skillful distorter of thinking processes is the writer of detective stories, crime yarns, or whodunits. His peculiar skill is in misleading the reader and causing him to give attention to a whole group of suspects only to find to his chagrin that the real murderer was the benevolent country doctor who never once had the slightest shadow of suspicion over him.

The successful crime writer achieves success by his misleading communications, but he is writing about a fictional world

to entertain his readers. In the important business of family
living we cannot afford such luxuries and must make every
effort to remove Type A Distortions.

Far too many people who pride themselves on being rational
individuals make many of the decisions about family relationships on a completely irrational basis. A man divorced his wife
on the grounds of incompatibility. He decided to make his
next choice far more wisely and enlisted the aid of a computer
service. He listed his requirements for the perfect mate on one
form and minutely described himself on another. The computer went to work and reviewed the material provided by
thirty thousand women and at last spewed out its recommendations. There were four women who seemed most suitable. At
the top of this list was the name of his ex-wife. Rationality had
apparently played little part in this evaluation of a marriage
relationship.

The Italians are generally considered emotional rather than
intellectual in their affairs of heart, but in the town of
Marostica the citizenry biannually show another side of the
issue by reenacting a legendary event in their town's history.
It had long been the custom of two contenders for a lady's
hand to fight a knightly contest to the death. In the year 1454,
Taddeo Parisio, governor of this city, decided to have done
with the bloodshed of knightly encounters and ordered the
contenders for his daughter's hand to play a game of chess.
To allow the townspeople to follow the game, Parisio had the
piaza in front of the castle marked off into squares and citizens
dressed to become living chessmen. Veri da Vallorama out-
maneuvered his opponent, won the match, and gained the
hand of the fair Lionaro.

Strange as the event might seem to modern minds, it at least
involved some thinking. We can only hope moderns would
bring at least as much thought to the important business of
marriage and family life and help to remove Type A Distortions.

The exhortation so significant in the plan to help an alcoholic through his problem is just as important in marriage and
family life—Think, Think, Think.

────── OVER ──→ TO ──→ YOU ──────

The "I always thought" in this chapter points up a fundamental weakness in many marriages. The parties to the marriage do not really know what they're getting into. One way to avoid this trap is to set up a contract before marriage so that both partners know what is expected of them. The following is the way one couple did it:

PREMARTIAL CONTRACT OF
JAMES GALLOWAY AND ROSEMARY CURTIS

James and Rosemary have talked at length and decided on the following guidelines for their marriage relationship:

Believing a Christian commitment is highly significant, both have decided to belong to and attend the same church. At the moment they are looking toward being members of First Methodist Church but may reconsider this later on. However, the principle will be that they'll both belong to the same church.

Money management will be their joint responsibility, but Rosemary will accept the task of writing the checks and reconciling the account. Both James and Rosemary will have certain pocket money which they can spend without explaining to each other.

Because James and Rosemary want good relationships with their in-laws, they agree to visit with each set of parents at least once a month. If there is any problem of communicating with either set of in-laws, it will be through the relation of James to his parents, Rosemary to hers.

Rosemary is going to keep on with her job. The present intention is for her to continue for at least three years or until the birth of a child when the situation will be reevaluated.

Because Rosemary will continue to work, James realizes that even though he has no real love of housework he will accept some definite, specific domestic responsibilities.

Realizing sex is an important factor in marriage and that men and women have distinctive sexual needs, James and Rosemary commit themselves to be thoughtful of each others needs and undertake to spend time constructively discussing their sexual relationship.

James and Rosemary plan to have two children and have with their physician agreed on the contraceptive method they will use.

_____

James Galloway

_____

Rosemary Curtis

This particular contract is very simple. You can make contracts just as elaborate and specific as you wish. However, beware of minutiae that may complicate and become too restrictive.

2. Suiting Up Your Thoughts

*Type B Distortions: Problems in Finding
Suitable Words with
Which to Express Your
Thoughts*

What do Humpty Dumpty and Mr. Shram, the father of three, have in common?

Mr. Shram has been having trouble getting his ideas across to his kids and says, "Can't you understand plain English? I just say what I mean and mean what I say."

Humpty Dumpty enunciated a similar idea. "When I use a word it means just what I choose it to mean—neither more than less."

Neither Mr. Shram nor Humpty Dumpty really realize the same word can have many different meanings for different people.

So high was the infant mortality rate in ancient times that it has been said the main hazard to life was being born. A similar condition exists in the field of interpersonal communications. A message may be formulated in one person's mind, but will it come to birth? If it is born, what condition will it be in?

Before it can be communicated, an idea must be translated into some other form, an activity sometimes referred to by the technical word *encoding*. The most frequently utilized means of encoding is to change the idea into words or sounds. Though this seems a simple activity, it is actually a complicated operation. Seldom do our verbalizations really accurately convey the ideas in our minds—what we say doesn't always convey what we think.

One of the most ambitious communication efforts ever made by man beautifully illustrates some of the problems of encoding. As the *Pioneer 10* spacecraft soared aloft from Cape Kennedy on its voyage to the space beyond the solar system, it carried a six-by-nine-inch plaque, anodized with erosion resistant gold, upon which was engraved what has now come to be known as a "message from earth."

The creator of this message from earth, Carl Sagan, is America's leading researcher into the science of exobiology—the study of extraterrestrial life. Sagan, in typical scientific fashion, says about such planets as Mars that he doesn't have a strong impression that there is life on Mars or a strong impression that there isn't life on Mars. He simply says it's time to go and find out.

This astronomer's theory so impressed the National Space Agency that they granted him their Medal for Scientific

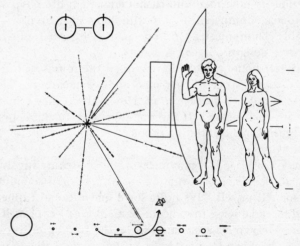

The pictorial plaque on *Pioneer 10* portraying the message from earth.

Achievement. When it came time to launch *Pioneer 10*, Sagan persuaded NASA officials to attach an aluminum plate that would carry a message for other civilizations living on distant heavenly bodies. The plate, as seen in the illustration, was engraved with mathematical and astronomical symbols believed to be understandable to any other civilization, in addition to the drawing of a human couple.

As a footnote, we may notice the message has been described as "Intergalactic Esperanto" and is said, in the words of the NASA release, to be "designed to show scientifically educated inhabitants of some other star system—who might intercept it millions of years from now—when Pioneer was launched, from where, and by what kind of beings."

In a test, a copy of this plaque was shown to over one hundred people, all college graduates, some with doctor's degrees, and not one of them was able to decipher the message. We could speculate that the residents of another planet who rushed over to pick up the remains of *Pioneer 10* would see the plate and excitedly take it to their scientific authorities. These learned individuals might well conclude that earthlings were nudists—the men, muscle-bound weight-lifter types and the women, dumpy little gals with long straight hair—who probably communicated with one another by means of strange geometric designs, circles, and dots.

Another thought might have crossed the minds of the residents of outer space: "That man and woman in the plaque are trying to get a message to us. How well do they communicate with each other?" If the question were further pursued, they'd discover the encoding problems which give rise to Type B Distortions.

When a message is communicated, the procedure involves at least two people. I may ruminate—intrapersonal communication—or tell myself, "It's quite lucid and rational to me; it's bound to make sense to someone else." But as I express it, the words so clear to me are just noises on the air. On one occasion I lost my wife in a German railroad station and rushed around asking people if they had seen her, but they just looked dumbly at me. We spoke different languages, and even those who knew English found it difficult to understand my frantic statements. The sounds I send out on the air must make sense to the person who hears them. There must be agreement between the speaker and the recipient as to what the words mean. I transmit sounds, vibrations on the air. A message is only really passed between two people when the recipient's decoding matches the sender's encoding.

The case of Bill and Susan Woffard is an instance of the Type B Distortion that interferes with husband-wife conversations. The Woffards are an average couple and feel they have a "good" marriage, but as time has passed, they have discovered a few areas in which they irritate each other. The type of TV programs each prefers becomes one of those sensitive points.

Susan is very fond of a variety of TV programs but is particularly interested in police and detective stories. She is a real whodunit nut, and when "Police Patrol" or "Super Sleuth" appear on the video tube, she gives the "one-eyed monster" her undivided attention.

Bill, normally easy going and tolerant of his wife's idiosyncrasies, finds her penchant for police stories somewhat irritating. While he spends a fair proportion of his own evenings before what he derisively calls the "boob tube," he is drawn toward football, baseball, and basketball and cannot stand the suspense of the police and detective programs so dear to his wife's heart. They just stir him up and make him feel uneasy.

The interpersonal marital communication experience starts when Bill decides in his mind that as two rational human beings he and Susan should sit down and discuss the matter of TV viewing cooly and impartially. In his mind, Bill rehearses the speech he plans to make.

"Honey, we are a couple of mature adults, and it is so silly that we irritate and worry each other over trivial matters. I think we should discuss this matter of the programs we view on TV. With the new season coming up it seems as if we should have a rational approach to TV viewing.

"As you know, I love football while you want to see 'Police Patrol,' and this will get us into a difficult situation on Monday nights. There are several lines of action we can take:

"(1) You can agree to let me see football on Mondays, and I'll let you choose the programs on Tuesday, Wednesday, and Thursday.

"(2) You could buy me a portable TV for my birthday, and I'll go into the bedroom to watch football while you see your program."

This was the way Bill planned in his "information source"—his brain—but he had to get the message across a distortion point to his "transmitter"—his vocal mechanism—which is no easy task.

Susan began to wonder when Bill offered to help with the dishes, and her suspicion of something pending was strengthened as he made some complimentary remarks about the meal they had just consumed.

BILL: I've been wondering if we could do something about this addiction of yours for detective programs on TV.

SUSAN: What do you mean "my addiction"?

Bill's statement just didn't "come out" right, and in short order he and Susan were attacking each other.

I am a great admirer of people who can come up with witty responses. I love the story of Ben Johnson. A man walked up to him and said, "So you're the famous Ben Johnson. You don't look as if you'd say boo to a goose."

The noted wit looked at his interlocutor for a moment, then responded, "Boo."

How I'd love to make statements like that. I do have a certain facility in the area and have an unusual knack for composing some of the wittiest responses—an hour after the conversation and in my mind. But when the opportunity presents itself again I come up with a ho-hum, so-so comment. What I think and what I say are different matters.

Then there's the problem of being tactful. Anyone with a modicum of sensitivity thinks about his statements and tries to avoid being a Jack Blunt. So when we seek to pass on a message, we dress it up a little. Our problem is that in the process of encoding we may obscure the thought we really want to transmit.

During World War II the FBI struggled with the formidable

task of tracking down the intelligence operations of a large number of German spies. The heart of the problem lay in discovering the techniques by which the operatives were transmitting their information to German headquarters.

A monumental breakthrough came with the discovery that the most important part of a whole page of writing was the dots over the *i*'s. These dots were the heart of the celebrated microdot system developed by Professor Zapp of the Dresden Institute of Technology. A message on a full sheet of paper was first reduced to the size of a postage stamp, then photographed through a reversed miscroscope which shrunk it to the size of a dot on a typewriter's *i*. The operator used a nipped-off hypodermic needle to lift and place the dot over an *i* in the text, after which it was cemented in place with a dab of collodion.

FBI agents discovered the secret while viewing a suspect document. The light struck the surface at an angle, revealing what was described as "a punctuation period no bigger than a fly speck." Lifted from the paper and placed under a powerful microscope, the dot revealed a page of typewritten enemy information.

What J. Edgar Hoover called "the enemy's masterpiece of espionage" provides us with a beautiful example of a Type B Distortion. The real message is hidden beneath a flood of acceptable verbiage by which we try to work around the less palatable message.

Hidden messages are another variety of Type B's, as is seen in the interchange between a woman reporter and the governor of Wyoming. At a press conference in Cheyenne, the reporter questioned Governor Stanley Hathaway about the transfer of funds. At one point she asked, "Is it proper to rob Patricia to pay Pauline?"

Although the question ostensibly focused on finances, the use of "Patricia to pay Pauline" instead of the traditional "Peter to pay Paul" got across the reporter's femininist message.

Type B's are also found in the *ambivalent messages* husbands and wives pass on to each other. The problem comes when a spouse wants to get a message across to a mate. Not wishing to come straight out and say it, he gives off two messages—what he feels will be acceptable to his helpmate and what he really thinks.

Mrs. Market has news for her husband. "Mother would like us to spend our vacation with them this year. Don't you think that would be a good idea?"

Bob Market replies, "That's fine, so kind of her to invite us. My problem is that the boss says I may have to delay my vacation this year. It's not at all certain, but there's just enough doubt to make it impossible for me to make specific plans. Of course, if you'd like to go on your own . . ."

Bob is telling his wife that he doesn't want to upset her but he's not going to his in-laws for the vacation. This type of communication is sometimes referred to as a "double message" and wreaks havoc with interpersonal communication.

Language itself may bring its quota of Type B Distortions. Groups of people develop their own distinctive vocabulary.

I am thinking of good friend Sausage Kennedy who, despite his rather mundane name and humble station in life, was devoted to his little sister. He addressed the tiny one, " 'ook at 'oo're ickle finger . . . 'oo are a bootiful girl."

In answer to my inquiry he responded, "They don't understand adult talk; that's why you have to use baby language."

Sausage Kennedy was saying that if we want to communicate we must imitate the language the subject speaks. As a migrant to the United States who has what is called an "accent," I can tell you that people who reply to me by imitating my accent have one notable effect on me—they irritate and annoy me no end.

An adolescent often turns the table on the adult world by patronizingly using their language when talking with them while developing a lingua franca widely known and used by his peers.

A puzzled adult has versified a reaction:

> Remember when hippie meant big in the hips,
> And a trip involved travel in cars, planes and ships?
> When pot was a vessel for cooking things in,

And hooked was what grandmother's rug might have been?
When fix was a verb that meant mend or repair,
And "be-in" meant simply existing somewhere?
When neat meant well organized, tidy and clean,
And grass was a ground cover, normally green?
When lights and not people were switched on or off,
And the pill might have been what you took for a cough?
When camp meant to quarter outdoors in a tent.
And pop was what the weasel went?
When groovy meant furrowed with channels and hollows.
And birds were winged creatures, like robins and swallows?
When fuzz was a substance that's fluffy, like lint
And bread came from bakeries, not from the mint?
When square meant a ninety degree angled form
And cool was a temperature not quite warm?
When roll meant a bun, and rock was a stone,
And hang-up was something you did to a phone?
When chicken meant poultry, and bag meant a sack,
And junk, trashy cast-offs and old bric-a-brac?
When jam was preserves that you spread on your bread.
And crazy meant balmy, not right in the head?
When cat was a feline, a kitten grown up,
And tea was a liquid you drank from a cup?
When swinger was someone who swings in a swing,
And pad was a soft sort of cushiony thing?
When way-out meant distant and far, far away,
And a man couldn't sue you for calling him gay?
When dig meant to shovel and spade in the dirt;
And put-on was something you would do with a shirt?
When tough described meat too unyielding to chew,
And making a scene was a rude thing to do?
Words once so sensible, sober, and serious,
Are making the freak scene like psychedelirious.
It's groovy, man, groovy, but English it's not,
Me thinks that the language has gone straight to pot.

Within the family the most dramatic experience with unusual word forms generally comes with the discovery that the
children are using "gutter" or "locker-room" language. The
use of this language provides one of the strangest aspects of
encoding.

Gutter, or locker-room language, apparently fulfills a number of functions.

(1) *Gutter language may be an underground language.* In *Forbidden Love* Jeff Johnson tells about his experience in "gay circles" where homosexuals attending a social gathering would talk to each other using words in a way in which only they understood. The square people at the gathering would have no idea what they were talking about as they bandied around ideas one to another.

Gutter language may serve a similar purpose as a type of underground language used by a group of people who feel they can communicate with one another without the "establishment" or "squares" knowing what is being said. To further complicate the situation, much commonly used gutter language accuses the subject of violations of middle-class values, incest, illegitimacy, and so on. The speaker is apparently telling his subject, "You breaker of middle-class standards—you don't amount to much."

(2) *Gutter language can be a weapon of attack.* At the height of the student riots just a few years ago rebellious students showed their contempt of the establishment by using objectionable language. What began as the Free Speech Movement turned into the "Dirty Speech" Movement, with some protagonists standing on platforms shouting out what are generally referred to as four-letter words. One observer noticing long hair, dirty clothes, and bare feet commented, "They know every four-letter word except terms like *comb* and *soap.*" Their dress, like their language, was aimed at shocking people.

(3) *Gutter language provides a vehicle for catharsis.* At the moment of frustration many people feel the need for some violent expression, and apparently the use of some forbidden word helps them get it off their chest. In much the same way as a person will say "darn" or "foot" or "horsefeathers," there are some others who must use gutter language before they can really express their emotions.

(4) *Gutter language may indicate a poor vocabulary.* This possibility is seen in the statement, "Strong language may indicate weak thinking." The speaker may have such a limited

vocabulary that he uses these well-known words to express himself. They come to mind without having to give any thought to them. As one has said, "The profane person may not so much need a Bible as a dictionary."

The Bible is very clear as it cuts through the pretentions of gutter language. It says, "Above all, my brothers, never swear an oath, neither by heaven nor by earth nor by anything else; let your 'yes' be a plain 'yes,' your 'no' a plain 'no' lest you come into judgment" (James 5:12, Moffatt). The command to Christians once again makes it clear that gutter language is to have no part in a Christian's communication: "Dirty stories, foul talk, and coarse jokes—these are not for you" (Eph. 5:4, Living Bible). Gutter language should be treated with the contempt it deserves.

Many a mother is shocked when junior comes in and delivers a few four-letter words or when she comes across a secret note from Marilyn's friend sprinkled with this type of language. Most parents have been through this at some time or another. Stay calm, mother, and tell Marilyn in an even tone, "We use plain English and don't go in for gutter language. I understand gutter language, but we don't need to use it in our family."

Yet another Type B Distortion is seen in people who feel talking and communication are synonyms and that the amount of words determines the level of communication. *Space-filler* words are used by the speaker who has little intention of communicating an intrinsic meaning. Space fillers fulfil several other purposes.

TRICKS WITH ENCODING

Mr. Osborn is not feeling at his best. He has spent two harrowing hours in the dentist's chair and left with the admonition ringing in his ears, "Please don't eat anything for three or four hours, and with that anesthetic you probably won't be able to speak, which is just as well. I don't want anything to upset that dressing I've applied."

Despite this traumatic experience Mr. Osborn decided to join the Thursday luncheon group, and by means of a series of nonverbal gestures conveyed his message about the oral surgery. His companions' friendly chatter and good-natured ribbing did little to elevate his spirits.

When the waitress distributed the checks, he found himself in possession of a missive indicating he had consumed a bacon and lettuce and tomato sandwich and a cup of coffee for which he owed the sum of $2.15.

Mr. Osborn picked up the check to write a response only to discover one very small space of white on the document. He thought for a moment, then wrote down:

$$1\,0\,2\,0\,0\,4\,1\,8\,0$$

What was Mr. Osborn saying?

I ought to owe nothing for I ate nothing.

Some space-fillers are just that. They convey no information but fill in some space. One troubled girl sat telling her story. Every few words were punctuated with "and stuff." "This girl moved out and stuff." "I went to the employment agency. They asked me to fill out a form and stuff." A secretary used a similar device with the word *everything*. "I had to do all this typing and everything." "I went to the staff meeting and everything."

One particularly annoying space-filler is "you know." A young professional footballer interviewed after a game in which he was the hero related his experience and periodically punctuated it with "you know." "I ran, you know, then I saw a receiver open, you know, then I threw the ball, you know, and he caught it, you know . . ." Whenever I am listening to someone with this habit, I feel as if I want to respond, "If I know, why are you telling me?" The answer would be academic. He isn't concerned whether I knew or not. He is filling a space.

Another variant is the frequently heard "and-uh." These "and-uhs" punctuated through the statement serve the purpose of giving the speaker time to prepare for the next statement and are a warning signal—"Don't start responding; there's more to come."

Space-fillers may be a bluff. A graduate student makes a statement: "The correlation between these two factors is not significant, etc., etc." "One group worked to help him face his domestic responsibility, etc., etc." The speaker is saying in effect, "I have all sorts of other information I could pass on, but it can't be done at the moment." A similar device is the use of such phrases as "and so on," "so forth," to convey the impression of a vast store of knowledge the speaker has available but doesn't have time to express.

The Romans used to say, "Repetition is the mother of learning," and more modern sages have expressed the same concept as "repetition breeds retention." Many a wife and mother trying to get an idea across to her husband or children has intuitively used the principle with something less than satisfactory results. The person who launches a verbal bombardment has some vague notion that the quantity of speech will overwhelm and convince, but it is seldom effective.

One peculiarity of the U.S. Senate is the phenomenon of the filibuster. Utilizing this legislative tactic, a senator or a group of senators opposed to a bill under consideration talk on ad infinitum until weary colleagues despair and drop the offensive legislation. Senator Strom Thurmond once discoursed for twenty-four hours and eighteen minutes, and a team effort, aimed at the Civil Rights Bill of 1964, created a record by holding the floor for seventy-two days. Much of this talk was frequently completely irrelevant. When Senator Huey Long was holding the floor, he included the recipe for "potlikker," and some filibusterers have resorted to such tactics as reading telephone directories, the World Almanac, a treatise on butterfly anatomy, and Aesop's Fables. There is much speech, many words, but these are obstructionist tactics, and there's no real attempt at communication.

Beethoven is credited with saying a musical composition must have two elements—familiarity and uniqueness. The same principle applies to most communicable material. Information completely new and unfamiliar can frustrate the listener and fail to catch his interest. People love the familiar.

For example, children delight in requesting the oft-repeated story and adore joining in at known climactic points. An adult responds automatically to the well-known tune.

However, let a message be too familiar, and it becomes boring and calls for responses such as "I kicked the bottom out of my cradle when I first heard that," or a derisive gesture indicating the information is old and bewhiskered.

Which leads us to the communication technique known as *nagging*. Nagging fails as a communication technique because of the familiarity of the material.

The word *nag* has been defined as, "To torment by persistent fault-finding, complaints, or importunities," and the Oxford Dictionary further adds to the definition and says it means "to gnaw, bite, nibble." Many families do not enjoy this torment and become defensive and fight back. In one family whenever mother introduced certain ideas, the whole family would commence to sing, "Tell Me the Old, Old Story." So mother's good intentions were continually frustrated. Strangely enough, she often felt she was being martyred. In that sense she gained something out of the experience but achieved nothing as far as communications were concerned.

If you are tempted to nag, here are some hints as to the way you can avoid this pitfall.

(1) Don't make a predictable response.

(2) Remember, no matter what satisfaction it gives you, nagging has a negative influence on your family, so you've accomplished nothing.

(3) Be subtle. Get your idea across in as many different ways as you can.

(4) Acknowledge that you don't know everything and that you could just be wrong.

(5) Build the logic of your ideas so the family will be able to reach some conclusions of their own.

(6) Don't gloat when logic proves you to be correct.

The amount of verbiage is by no means an index of the way we are communicating. Pliny the Elder on one occasion admitted, "I am writing you at length because I do not have time to write a short letter." It has been pointed out that the

Lord's Prayer, the Gettysburg Address, the Declaration of Independence, and a government directive on cabbage prices require 56, 266, 300, and 29,911 words respectively.

Another category of Type B Distortions is seen in the person who possesses what has been called a fatal fluency.

Peter Harrison was in trouble. Gifted with a native verbal facility, he had little formal education but was such an attractive speaker that people flocked to hear him preach in church. In middle life well-meaning friends persuaded him to enroll in seminary, but he never quite adjusted to the unaccustomed discipline of an academic setting.

After Peter had preached a sermon to the preaching class, the professor rose to comment: "Mr. Harrison, you undoubtedly have a native speaking gift, but your words come out like a torrent. I would suggest you slow down and clothe your thoughts with more appropriate language."

The irrepressive Peter immediately replied, "The trouble is, professor, the little beggars pop out before I can get their shirts on."

So many of us are like Peter, and there's all the difference in the world between thoughts and expressed words.

In the interpersonal communications between husband and wife Type B Distortions represent the difference between what a spouse thinks and what is actually enunciated.

If you think you have trouble putting your thoughts into words, consider the case of Lana and be thankful. This sweet little girl's vocal cords had never developed like a normal human's; consequently, she was unable to speak. An interested scientist decided to help Lana overcome her difficulty and enlisted the aid of a team of specialists including a linguist, a biochemical engineer, an electronics technician, and a behavioral researcher. They combined their talents and mounted a team effort to teach the girl to speak through a machine. At last report, Lana had mastered a seventy-five-word vocabulary and was actually putting words into sentences which she communicated by pushing keys on a computer.

Not bad considering Lana is a three-and-a-half-year-old chimpanzee.

If these scientists can spend all this time, money, and effort in an attempt to teach a chimpanzee to punch out the message, "Please, machine, give piece of banana period," surely humans must work harder at honing their capacity to put their thoughts into words, avoiding the distortions that can impair our communication skills.

―――――― OVER ⟶ TO ⟶ YOU ――――――

Look back on page 25 at the "Message from Earth." Puzzled? Join the crowd.

Below is the official interpretation of the plaque's inscription. Read it through.

"The radiating lines at left represent the positions of 14 pulsars—cosmic sources of radio energy—arranged to indicate our Sun as the home star of the launching civilization. The '1—' symbols at the ends of the lines are binary numbers that represent the frequencies of these pulsars at the time of the launch of Pioneer F relative to that of the hydrogen atom shown at the upper left with a '1' unity symbol. The hydrogen atom is thus used as a 'universal clock', and the regular decrease in the frequencies of the pulsars will enable another civilization to determine the time that has elapsed since Pioneer F was launched. The hydrogen atom is also used as a 'universal yardstick' for sizing the human figures and outline of the spacecraft shown on the right. The hydrogen wavelength—about 8 inches—multiplied by the binary number representing '8' shown next to the woman give her height—64 inches. The figures represent the type of creature that created Pioneer. The man's hand is raised in a gesture of goodwill. Across the bottom are the planets, ranging outward from the Sun, with the spacecraft's trajectory arcing away from Earth, passing Mars, and swinging by Jupiter."

Does this explanation clarify the meaning of the message for you? If you do not have a scientific background, there's a good chance the "encoding" of the message beat you and helps you to understand the problem of putting ideas into words.

3. The Way You Say It Makes the Difference

Type C1 Distortions: Difficulties in Getting Your Message Across

Henrietta Simpson is pouring out a tearful story to her mother. Mrs. Stacey, for her part, has never suspected there might be difficulties in her daughter's marriage. Though anxious to be loyal to her own flesh and blood, she inwardly wonders if her daughter may not be exaggerating the situation.

Mrs. Stacey is particularly bothered by the vague lament, "I never thought he would talk to me like that," and she queries, "Tell me exactly what Tom said."

Henrietta dabs her tears and responds, "It wasn't so much what he said as the hateful way he said it."

Henrietta has run upon the technique whereby the meaning of a statement can be changed by the manner in which it is spoken.

Amid the colorful stories of the Old Testament none is more fascinating for the student of communication than that of a peculiar situation following a battle between the men of Gilead and the Ephraimites.

Jephthah, leader of the Gileadites, had bottled up the Ephraimites and gained control of the Jordan River crossings that provided the only way of escape. His problem was to distinguish friend from foe as they forded the river. He discovered a simple answer in the speech peculiarity of the Ephraimites who were unable to enunciate the *sh* sound.

As each man came across the ford claiming he was a Gileadite, he was asked to repeat *shibboleth*, the Hebrew word for corn. If the fugitive responded with *sibboleth*, he was immediately recognized as an Ephraimite.[1]

The dictionary today defines the word *shibboleth* as a "password," but this entails a misunderstanding of the original incident. The importance lay not in the word as a word but rather the way in which the word was pronounced. It was not a test of knowledge of a particular word but a check of the individual's capacity to enunciate correctly.

The mode of expression always plays a vital role in communication.

I have had some bad experiences in taking meals in fancy eating places where ordering by the menu descriptions is a hazardous process I like to dub "restaurant roulette." I read, "Fluffy golden omelette made from three country fresh grade AA eggs." Then comes a flat, sorry-looking, greasy lump of yellow which makes me want to say, "Is that a fluffy, golden omelette?"

It seemed the Royal Household Cafeteria was the answer to my problem. The food is top quality. I see it displayed, and I can be selective, putting together the sort of meal that will satisfy my appetite, conform to my diet, and fit my budget.

The Royal Household certainly knows how to display their food, coordinating the colors, cleverly arranging the dishes, garnishing the borders, decorative fruits, just the right lighting. Behind each of these islands of gastronomic delight stands a presiding assistant neatly clad in black dress with just the right relief of white at apron and collar. And herein is my problem. The assistant is the serpent in this Eden of luscious food.

The high priestess of the vegetable section is a nice-looking, middle-aged woman whose face has set into a sort of sneer. As a patron approaches, she says with her mouth, "Can I help you?" Before she is finished placing the meager piece of broccoli on his plate, she intones, "What else, please?" But the automatic, bored manner of address and the tone of her voice say, "For goodness sake, hurry on," while the pained look on her face fairly shouts, "Only one vegetable—what a cheapskate."

The problem here is that though the message coming from the brain may be successfully put into words, the way it is transmitted determines whether or not the message will be received.

Joseph Conrad, skillful craftsman of literature and wizard in the use of words, is credited with saying, "Give me the right word and the right accent, and I will move the world." Communication does not exist in words alone. The manner in which the message is transmitted can make all the difference.

The way in which a method of expression makes a message more palatable was demonstrated by the techniques of a gifted psychotherapist who worked in therapy groups using confrontational methods. He masked his incisive mind behind an engaging smile. As the session progressed, the time came for him to do some confronting, and he launched into the process of facing a group member with some negative aspect of his adjustment to life.

The therapist turned his beaming countenance upon the subject and, in a voice sounding for all the world like a fond parent expressing loving disappointment, made the frankest statements: "That certainly was a childish action to take." "You have obviously been very irresponsible." "You didn't show up too well there." All of this he did with his face wreathed in a winning smile. Very seldom did anybody take umbrage at the statements that would have normally made them hopping mad. The expression on his face and the note of concern in his voice made all the difference in passing on the message.

The role of methods of speaking in communication gives family members a clue to a strategy for communicating critical or unacceptable message to others in the family group. Let us take the difficult case of saying *no*—a short important, yet difficult message that must on occasions be passed on within a family.

Synanon, a self-help group that has chalked up an outstanding record in working with drug addicts, claims that the best way to help a person in great difficulty is to turn upon him with a specific dogmatic chorus of "no . . . no . . . no . . . no . . ."2

When the addict first arrives at the Synanon House, he is met with a chorus of no's. The leader tells the new member, "We are in the business of saying no. That's our business."

"Pretty soon we expect you to say, 'I want to visit my sister.' " *No!*

"I want five bucks." *No!*

"I want to go to the movies." *No!*

"I want to shoot dope." *No!*

"You know, that's the business we're in. We're going to tell you no for a long time. Pretty soon you're going to find that there is nothing in the world that you really can't do."

Note the order: Learn *no* and discover "There's nothing in the world that you really can't do."

Probably the most negative of all statements concerning human conduct is to be found in the Ten Commandments. At the bidding of Moses, the people made special preparation by washing their clothes and refraining from sexual activity for two days prior to the special event. They staked out Mount Sinai with strict orders that neither man nor beast was to go beyond the boundaries.

As the Children of Israel gathered at the boundaries, the mountain presented an awesome spectacle, enshrouded in a black cloud, lightning flashing, the ground heaving in an earthquake, and a blast of sound assaulting the Israelites' ears. When Moses descended from the mountain, he carried stone tablets in his arms and announced they were inscribed by the finger of God.

Approaching Moses, the leaders of the people said, "Behold, the Lord our God hath shewed us his glory and his greatness, and we have heard his voice out of the midst of the fire" (Deut. [King James] 5:24). The accompanying cloud, fire, earthquake, voice raised the effectiveness of the message. The way in which this negative message was transmitted to the Children of Israel made sure that it would be impressed upon their hearts as being of great moment.

Of course it is much more difficult with human relationships. Except to the most hardened it is always a problem to say no. A professional football player was talking with a new recruit who asked what chance he had of making the team. The footballer replied, "Two chances." Then in a softer voice he added, "Slim and none at all."

Saying no will never be easy, but some simple techniques can help take the pain out of the process.

Remove the refusal from the personal basis. Make it clear that while you appreciate the other person and his request, because of the premises under which you are operating, you must refuse.

Indicate that you don't enjoy saying no. Take it gently. Work the conversation around to a moment when you say, "Nothing would please me more than to go along with you, and I hate to do it, but I must say no."

Give evidence that you have studied the situation. Don't convey the impression that this is an arbitrary, ill-considered decision. Comment on the considerations that entered into denying the request.

Help him say no to himself. Show him the factors involved in such a way that he may reach the negative conclusion before you break the news to him.

Suggest some factors which might have changed the no to yes. Explain some of the considerations and proceed: "Now if the situation had been . . ." " If your request had . . ." "But you realize . . ."

Help him see the situation from your perspective. Try to show him how it looks from a viewpoint other than his: "If you were in my place, what would you do?"

Preeminently let your no be said in the nicest way. Let your expressive skills work for you. Speaking of the president of a great institution, one of his employees said, "He sometimes refused my requests, but he did it so kindly and graciously that I never felt upset by his refusal." This is the way to do it.

Why not try rehearsing saying no. Stand and look at yourself in a mirror and make your refusal. How do you come across? Try it again. Convey your negatives tactfully, gently, and courteously, and you will have mastered a significant facet of communication.

Despite all these possibilities of improving the communication by the way in which a message is expressed, family members frequently miss their opportunity and mess things up with a Type C1 Distortion.

There's a good chance the lady in the cafeteria, presiding over the vegetables and mentioned in the opening of this chapter, may be particularly competent because she has been practicing Type C1 Distortions at home. Husbands and wives are frequently past masters of the art of using a polite courteous term to convey something less than a courteous message.

It takes practice for a married person to learn to address his spouse as "hon——eee," "darl——ing," or "sweethear-r-r-t" in such a way as to bring out the last syllable like the crack of a whip. In this way the term of endearment will carry a rebuke to a spouse. The language of love literally drips with venom.

A popular literary device is the use of irony—a statement says one thing on the surface but underneath means exactly the opposite. While irony may have a gentle teasing overtone, it may also bite. At this point Type C Distortion enters the picture, and by verbal expression the speaker transmits sarcasm.

Mr. Solomon, a hard-working accountant, sits looking over the report card brought home from school by his son Jimmy. His offspring, at this moment vividly aware of his poor showing, apprehensively awaits the paternal reaction. His father's words are laudatory: "You certainly make a father proud of his son." But the manner of expression tells the boy his father is disappointed and upset.

Husbands and wives often become experts in the art of verbal cut and nick called sarcasm. Mr. Taylor, gazing at the TV dinner just placed before him by his spouse, remarks, "You've obviously been taking a course in gourmet cooking."

Mrs. Briggs, who's been fussing at her husband for spending so much time playing poker, looks at the bonus check brought home by her spouse: "That's some bonus check, Harry."

A husband, aware of his wife's bridge-playing activities,

stands looking over the den: "I've gotta give it to you, Vera, you're a tremendous housekeeper."

Sarcasm is an example of Type C1 Distortions. The speaker makes a statement that by itself would have one meaning, but the manner of speech gives it the opposite significance. This method is geared to deliver a rapier thrust or cut and wound the recipient.

Yet another variation of Type C1 Distortions is the use of a technique generally called *teasing* or *kidding*. In this process the speaker makes a statement obnoxious to his receiver and, after making his point, retreats by saying, "I was only teasing."

Martin Luther's life gives us some beautiful examples of husband-wife relationships. When an artist painted Luther's portrait and wanted to know which was the reformer's best profile, his subject replied, "Paint me warts and all." This comment typifies Luther's relationship with his wife. The Luthers had a group of students living with them, and these guests recorded verbatim many of the interchanges between Martin and his wife, Katie.

One interchange shows Luther in a teasing mood.

LUTHER: We shall yet see the day when a man will take several wives.

KATIE: The devil thinks so.

LUTHER: The reason, dear Katie, is that a woman can have only one child a year, whereas a man can beget several.

KATIE: Paul says, "Let each man have his own wife."

LUTHER: Aye, his own wife, but not only one; that is not in Paul.

Thus the doctor joked a long time until Katie said: "Before I would stand for that I would go back to the convent and leave you and all your children!"[3]

Luther, who would fight to the death for the principle of monogamy, enjoyed teasing his wife about the alleged masculine bent toward polygamy.

Many teasers have a more specific goal in mind and will test

the situation by pushing things as far as they can before re-
treating. Teasing can develop into a subtle torture carried on
in public and causing the recipient intense silent agony. When
the victim finally turns, the adept teaser laughs it off with,
"I was only teasing." Teasing stands with sarcasm as one of the
cruelest Type C1 Distortions.

While visiting an overseas military installation, I sat at a
table eating a snack. On the other side were a father and son.
The father, trim and neat and clean-cut in his uniform, talked
with his carelessly clad son whose long flaxen locks hung like
a curtain around his face giving him quite an attractive but
distinctively feminine appearance. From their conversation it
soon became clear they were engaged in a father-son session
in which the boy was stymieing his father with Type C1 Distortions.

FATHER: What's all this foolishness about your wanting to
go away for the weekend?
(His offspring sat looking ahead and mumbled a few words.)
FATHER: Eh?
(The lad made a few more lip movements.)
FATHER: How's that?
(Once more a mumbled reply.)
FATHER: Who are you thinking of going with?
(The boy uttered a few vague sounds.)
SON: Some of the guys.
FATHER: How did you think you were going to travel?
(As if in a reverie the boy mumbled some type of response.)
FATHER: I suppose you said something.

The boy was controlling the whole situation by using a Type
C1 Distortion.

Sometimes Type C1 Distortions are just a matter of speech
mechanics. Don Lacey is one of those people who has the
erroneous idea that he can speak without opening his mouth.
Consequently, his conversation with Martha, his wife, has
suffered.

At first Martha used to say, "I can't hear you, dear."

Later it got to, "I wish you wouldn't mumble when you speak."

This latter remark with its implied criticism aggravated Don who would thereupon raise his voice to a level where it could certainly be heard and carried the message of his annoyance which left Martha reluctant to respond to his verbalizations.

Don's Type C1 Distortions were hindering their marital communications.

Hazel Clayton is another example. Petite and attractive, Hazel grew up in a home where her mother always emphasized that a lady is soft spoken and never raises her voice.

Hazel's verbal interchanges with her husband, Bill, always leave him in a state of uncertainty as to what she said, and in his irritation he's reluctant to ask her to "run that by again."

Of all the distortions in interpersonal communication, these Type C1's are theoretically the easiest to remedy. A series of sessions with a speech therapist or even a drama coach could bring the necessary change. But such is the vanity of the human spirit that few of us can really face the truth about our means of expression.

Transmissive techniques, that is, the way in which a message is expressed, have tremendous potentialities for improving the quality of communication, but they are also very vulnerable and susceptible to Type C1 Distortions which can complicate the process.

One writer in the field of communication reports an enlightening incident in the experience of Shannon, the distinguished formulator of one of the most respected of all communication theories. Wishing to hear how his theory sounded when expounded by someone else, the celebrated communication expert attended a lecture being given on the Shannon theory. He received a rude awakening. The lecturer stood gazing at the ceiling as he delivered an uninspiring utterance. One gets the impression Shannon might have been unconvinced about his own theory if this particular lecture had been his only exposure to it. A magnificent communication theory was completely distorted by the way an individual transmitted the message.

$$\longrightarrow \text{OVER} \longrightarrow \text{TO} \longrightarrow \text{YOU}$$

Here are some domestic situations where you may learn by making choices of responses.

(1) Your son Lionel wants to use the new automobile to take Patricia Wilson on a date. You have grave doubts about Lionel's driving prowess. How do you answer him?

[ ] a. "No way—not with your driving ability."

[ ] b. "I know how badly you want to use the car and I hate to say no, but I'm afraid I can't let you have it. Those two tickets you got last month scare me. When you earn a good record on the old car, I'll let you have the new one."

[ ] c. "I may want to use the car myself."

(2) Your wife is very fond of bridge. You feel it's an awful waste of time. She says, "The new president of the bank and his wife are having a bridge party, and they've invited us. Isn't that good?" You respond:

[ ] a. "Good? They're only out to get some new accounts at the bank."

[ ] b. "I suppose I'll have to go or you'll be nagging me about never going anywhere with you."

[ ] c. "Isn't that great? I'm thrilled about the invitation. It's a tribute to your popularity. I know you'll have a wonderful time but it would be misery for me. I'll catch up on fixing that back screen door while you are enjoying bridge."

(3) You and your husband have been to a dinner at Aunt Henrietta's house. Henrietta is a regular "duchess" and very stuffy about etiquette. Your husband knocked over the soup, and Henrietta made a face like a thundercloud. On the way home in the car you say:

[ ] a. "You certainly made me feel proud of you tonight, Harry, I'm sure Aunt Henrietta was impressed."

[ ] b. "Didn't you ever learn to hold the soup tureen with two hands?"

[ ] c. "You performed well in a difficult situation with that soup. I've been through experiences like that myself. We'll be able to laugh at it all one of these days."

ANSWERS

(1) Definitely "b." You show understanding, give reasons, and tell him how he can qualify in the future.
(2) The best reply is "c." You show understanding and a willingness to put yourself out by repairing the screen door.
(3) The only way is "c." Neither of the others will accomplish more than irritating your spouse.

4. Your Actions Speak So Loudly . . .

Type C2 Distortions: Problems Arising from the Difficulty in Understanding What Family Members are Saying by Their Body Movements

Masters and Johnson, the two foremost investigators into human sexuality in our day, have never sat down to *talk* to their children about the birds and bees. They prefer a nonverbal technique. One commentator notes: "Masters says the best home-style sex education is exposure to spontaneous warmth and affection between parents. 'There is nothing that teaches about sex half as much as Pop patting Mom's fanny as he walks by her in the kitchen. Obviously she loves it, and the kids watch and say, "Boy, that's for me." That's sex education as it can be done in the home.' "[1]

As with sex education, so much teaching within the family is carried on at a nonverbal level—one of the most fascinating methods used by one human to communicate with another.

What do Thomas Edison proposing to Nina Miller, a schoolboy raising his hand in class, and a bee returning to the hive show us about communication? They each demonstrate nonverbal communication.

Thomas Alva Edison's first wife, Mary Stillwell, died in 1884. Two years later he remarried—a marriage preceded by a most unusual courtship. By this time Edison had lost his hearing and developed skill in using Morse Code. As the relationship with Nina Miller grew, he taught her to use the code. Spending long periods of time together, they became adept at tapping out messages on each other's hands.

When Edison finally decided to "pop the question," he used the familiar Morse Code. Nina responded with what Edison called "an easy word to send by telegraphic signals—yes."

On their honeymoon trip, traveling by train through the White Mountains, Edison and his new bride carried on a sugary, newly wed, pet-name conversation despite the presence of three other people in the carriage. They accomplished this rather unusual feat by tapping out telegraphic code on each other's hands.

The schoolboy raising his hand in class is telling his teacher something. A bent and sagging arm says, "I'm tired of waiting to be called on"; a darting, stabbing motion, "Please, please, I'm certain I know it"; a tentative, uncertain, shy hand, "I'm trying to make a show but please don't call on me." Without ever opening his mouth the pupil is passing on a significant message to his teacher.

Bees returning to their hives were the subject of close investigation by Karl von Frisch, sharer of the 1973 Nobel Prize in medicine. It had long been known that bees communicated, but the process was not understood. Karl von Firsch, after a prolonged study, concluded the bees communicated by means of an intricate dance.

If the scout bee discovered honey within 160 feet of the hive, it performed a "round dance," moving in a circular motion, then pointing to the source of the nectar. When the supply of nectar was over 160 feet, the returning bee did a "wagging dance" before finally stepping forward to indicate the direction.

Edison with his bride, the schoolboy's arm motions, and the dance of the bees are all vivid demonstrations of nonverbal communication. This whole area opens up countless possibilities for sending ideas and emotions from one person to another.

Gestures may give us away by indicating what we really mean despite what our lips are saying. A study carried on by an Englishman some years ago compared what an individual was saying verbally with the nonverbal messages he was passing on. By comparing the two messages, he concluded that the nonverbal messages were far more truthful to the individual's ideas than were his verbal statements.

One report told of a news commentator who was making a laudatory statement about "today's youth," but even as he made the statements he put his index finger to the side of his nose and, according to this reporter, was nonverbally indicating either doubt about the statement or how his audience would respond.

All of this helps to strengthen the idea advanced by some communicators that nonverbal communication may be at least as important as verbal communication. Some researchers have concluded that in a normal, nonprofessional conversation the total message communicated is estimated at 55 percent facial, 38 percent vocal, and only 7 *percent verbal*. This may mean that more is being communicated nonverbally than verbally. Another expert claims that the average person only verbalizes a minuscule eleven to twenty-five minutes a day. (I know there are many exceptions; for myself, my total goes much higher than this. Imagine then how few words are spoken by those who lower the average.) All this means people are pouring out a torrent of information with eyes, eyebrows, facial expressions, hands, and bodily movements.

Body Language

It is a strange anomaly that as we have overcome many problems by technological advance our major difficulties have not been with the sophisticated machines but in the relationships between the masters who control them. Differences arise between employer and employee, seller and buyer, professional and client, parties in legal conflict, and between nation and nation.

In part to cope with some of these difficulties there has arisen a group among the ranks of managers who specialize in the delicate art of negotiating. Training these negotiators has been a complex and difficult task. The negotiator has to develop a capacity to understand his opposite number sitting on the other side of the table. He needs to know what that man is thinking, the issues upon which he is unmoveable, and where he is willing to bend a little.

As Gerald I. Nierenberg, author of *The Art of Negotiating*, says, "Negotiation depends on communication." This communication takes place in a number of different ways. To discover what his opposite number is seeking to gain from the negotiating process the negotiator must listen to what the man is saying with his mouth . . . and . . . his body.

Body?

Particularly with his body. With his mouth he is making statements to lead the other party astray. If the astute negotiator is to get the message as to what his opponent really wants, he must learn the language of gestures.

In part because of this necessity experts in negotiating have become proficient in reading the language of body movement. It had been recognized that movements of the body were conveying some sort of a message, but a bodily movement is a subtle, ephemeral thing. Unlike spoken language which can be written down on paper, there is no widely accepted way of making a record of bodily movements.

Experts in the field of negotiation tried to learn from their experiences by using video tape for recording their sessions. After video-taping some twenty-five hundred negotiating sessions these researchers were fascinated by the gestures used by the participants in the sessions. In a series of post-session evaluations by the participants they were able to discover a whole new gesture language.[2]

The researchers early discovered that in the same way as a word by its relationship to other words may take on new meanings, so gestures had to be considered in relationship to other gestures. They learned to look for gesture clusters in which a series of related gestures had a total meaning and were said to be congruent.

The accompanying chart is a summary of some of the meanings of gestures as discovered by researchers and should be read with caution, recollecting the importance of the "gesture cluster." Even with these qualifications, it soon becomes evident that the study of gestures opens up a fascinating new world.

While the most significant work in nonverbal communication has been done by video-taping these sessions of interchange between professional negotiators, there's a good chance they could have gathered just as much material in any good-sized family, particularly in its educational functions. Dr. Charles Galloway, national authority on the subject of body language, says, "Educators are multi-sensory organisms who only occasionally talk." The way the professor extends his arms or puts his hands in his pocket, nods his head, moves toward the class, looks class members in the eye, smiles at them, or walks down into the middle of the seats does much to determine the effectiveness of his teaching.

The same may be true in a family. Just watch a father as he gives his child an encouraging pat on the shoulder before he goes into the Little League game, or the way he throws his arms around him after a home run. Look at a mother observing her children in action. Like some professional coach sending in plays at the football game, she furrows a brow in warning, calls for a consultation with her bent first finger, nods her head in approval at a kind action, or slowly, menacingly swings the same head from side to side in a deliberate no. She may smile or wink approval, hold up a hand as authoritatively as any traffic policeman to call attention to a fault, or reduce the volume of sound wth a *sh-h-h* sign of a finger to the lips. The slap or swat carry their own peculiar nonverbal message.

On Being a Soft Touch

In earlier chapters we discussed the articulatory methods of transmitting messages by speech in the form of sound waves. In this chapter we have considered movements of the body, hands, arms, and face which travel in the form of light waves to be received by the eyes of the recipient.

A third way in which the message may be transmitted is by

tactile means, for example, a handshake or an embrace. These touching activities sometimes carry a message that could never be satisfactorily spoken.

I once served as the chaplain of a large army hospital where we had a fine dermatologist of Polish origin and training. While on rounds with him one day we stopped before a bad case of dermatitis. The nurse removed the dressings to show the badly infected skin. Without a moment's hesitation the dedicated doctor leaned over and began to rub his fingers over the infected spots. The onlookers were amazed, as was the patient. Smiling into the patient's face, the dermatologist assured him that everything was going to be all right. Back in his office later, I asked the doctor if it was his usual practice to touch the infected spots. He replied that in his medical training he had been taught never to show fear in the presence of infection. This confident attitude helped to quell the apprehensions of the patient.

These same methods are as effective with psychic as with physical suffering. In one therapy group the members will focus their attention on one of their numbers who is hurting and "reach out"—stretch out and touch him. The touch often helps to break down the feeling of isolation.

Family relationships are fostered by touch. It has long been known that babies have need of bodily contact; so do children, and as many people grow older, they have even greater needs for these contacts.

Distortions in Nonverbal Communication

All of this sounds so convincing that many people get the idea they can learn a whole set of gestures, postures, or grimaces and be able to read anyone they meet. However, distortions enter in and complicate nonverbal communication.

A series of studies has shown that people who cover their mouths while talking may be lying or unsure of themselves. But there is a possibility that the person may be like a friend of mine who has a rather bushy mustache, newly grown, and is fearful it may have gathered some mayonnaise while he was

BODY LANGUAGE

MOVEMENT	DESCRIPTION	POSSIBLE MEANING
SMILES: SIMPLE	Lips together, teeth unexposed	*Person is not participating in any outgoing activity, is smiling to himself.*
UPPER	Upper incisors exposed, usually with eye-to-eye contact between individuals	*A greeting smile when friends meet—or when children greet their parents.*
BROAD	Both upper and lower incisors exposed and eye-to-eye contact seldom occurs	*Associated with laughing, commonly seen during play.*
HOLDING HANDS	Two women gently hold the other's hands in theirs and with congruous facial expressions communicate their deep sympathy	*Woman's expression of sincere feelings to another woman during a crisis.*
OPEN HANDS	Palms up	*Sincerity and openness.*
CROSSED ARMS	Men—arms crossed on chest Women—arms crossed lower on body	*Defensiveness, defiance, withdrawal.*
LEG OVER CHAIR	Sits with one leg up over chair arm	*Indifference or hostility to other person's feelings or needs.*
LEG KICKING	Legs crossed with foot moving in a slight kicking motion	*Boredom.*
HAND TO CHEEK	"The Thinker" position with hand on cheek	*Involved in some sort of meditation.*
STROKING CHIN	Hand strokes chin—man strokes beard or mustache	*He is in process of making decision.*

BODY LANGUAGE

MOVEMENT	DESCRIPTION	POSSIBLE MEANING
GLASSES	Very slowly and deliberately takes glasses off and carefully cleans the lenses—or puts the earpiece of the frame in the mouth	*Procrastination—pausing for thought—gaining time to evaluate.*
PINCHING BRIDGE OF NOSE	Closes eyes, pinches bridge of nose	*May signal his self-conflict, quandary about a matter.*
SIDEWAYS GLANCE	Often takes a sideways position, body turned away	*Associated with distrusting attitude—a gesture of rejection.*
HANDS ON HIPS	Standing—Both hands placed on hips Sitting—Body leaning forward, one hand on knee	*Individual is goal-oriented —is ready and able.*
LEANING BACK HANDS SUPPORTING HEAD	Seated, leaning back, one leg crossed in figure-four position, both hands clasped behind head	*Gesture of superiority, smugness, and authority.*
JINGLING MONEY IN POCKET	Jingling coins in pocket	*May be much concerned with money or the lack of it.*
LOCKED ANKLES	Ankles crossed tightly, hands may also be clenched	*Holding back strong feelings and emotions—apprehension—tension.*
TUGGING EAR	Raises hand four to six inches, hand goes to earlobe, gives a subtle pull, then returns to its starting point	*An "interrupt gesture"—a signal of a wish to speak.*
STEEPLING	Joins finger tips and forms a "church steeple"	*Communicates idea he is very sure of what he is saying.*

eating his lunch. Consequently he rubs his hand over it periodically. The subject might even have had recent dental work or be the victim of advertising pressures that cause him to fear "bad breath."

Touching the nose is another good indication of a person's feelings. Wide studies have shown it generally means no while with an adolescent it may indicate "I don't know." There is another alternative—the subject may have an itching nose.

Gestures reveal sex. Only women walk toward each other and reach out to hold each other's hands. Women more than men cross their legs and move one foot with a rapid, kicking movement that generally indicates boredom. On the other hand, only American males sit with their legs crossed in a figure-four position.

The value of this may be that we can tell men from women. However, in all honesty we must admit there are easier ways to discover the sex of a person.

Even the most expert interpreters of nonverbal language admit there are many complications. Gestures have to be considered in clusters, or are said to be understood only when the gesture is congruent, that is, in the light of a number of other factors.

Yugoslavs who live in the part of their country known as Macedonia have a peculiar nonverbal technique for conveying yes or no. In the years of Turkish occupation the conquerors organized a massive effort to convert the Yugoslavs to the Mohammedan faith. Apprehending a native they would place a scimitar at his throat and ask, "Do you believe in Mohammed?"

The subject, vividly aware of his situation, would vigorously nod his head backwards and forwards in the universally accepted gesture to indicate yes. The response satisfied both parties because the wily Yugoslavs had agreed amongst themselves to reverse meanings. For them, turning the head sideways from left to right indicated yes while nodding backwards and forwards indicated no.

In nonverbal communication, more than in any other type,

both the sender and the receiver must agree on the meanings of the symbol.

A message between husband and wife may be communicated in a number of ways—a raised eyebrow, a wink, handing over flowers or candy, banging cupboards and slamming doors, a handshake, squeezing a hand, a kiss. Because it is nonverbal, this type of communication has a tremendous potential for misunderstanding.

A man and his wife were playing cards with some friends. After the cards had been dealt, the husband glanced up and saw his wife was obviously trying to tell him something by rolling her eyes and then looking in a peculiar manner down the side of her face. She seemed so intent on the process that he felt confident she had a good hand and was letting him know; so he bid accordingly.

Well, she had nothing in her hand, and they lost the game. Following the dealing of the next hand while their partners were intent on their cards, he saw she was obviously trying to get his eye again. This time she lifted her hand to her cheek.

Somewhat uncertain as to what this signal meant, the husband concluded that because it was different from the previous communication she was probably indicating she really had some good cards; so he bid enthusiastically. To his horror he discovered she had another sorry hand.

In the painful discussion which followed later, his wife disclosed that she was trying to tell him he had a piece of shaving cream on his right cheek. Unless there is basic agreement on the meaning of signs and symbols, nonverbal is the most vulnerable to distortions of all forms of communication.

One area of nonverbal communication with great potentiality is in the example parents provide for their children. We are learning the importance of imitative learning, a process whereby children easily learn to reproduce other people's behavior—particularly that of their parents.

I once lived in a rural area not far from an abandoned brick pit. At the bottom of the brick pit was a pool of water that attracted rabbits. I used to set a trap alongside of the pool, and each afternoon I'd take my little two-year-old son on my shoulders across the field. We'd climb the precipitous trail down the side of the pit to the pool at the bottom.

One wet, cold, wintry afternoon I decided to slip off from the house without my son to see if I had caught anything. Arriving at the pit I found the clay trail wet and slippery, and as I cautiously made my way down the slippery pathway, I began to feel increasingly apprehensive. About halfway down I stopped, holding onto a convenient tree limb and inwardly debating as to whether I should risk going any further.

As I stood there a stone rolled by, and I looked back up the trail to see my son toddling down toward me. I began to talk quickly, "Warwick, don't come any further, stay there, son . . ." Speaking as I moved, I gingerly climbed up to him. Picking him up in my arms I began the struggle up the path to the top of the pit.

Though it was a bitterly cold day, by the time I reached the top I was bathed in perspiration. A thought flashed through my mind: "That's the way it is, John Drakeford. Where you go, your son goes; where you place your feet, he places his."

Parents must be particularly careful about the sort of models their children imitate. Beginning with themselves, they should make sure they communicate a wholesome nonverbal message to their children.

```
───────────── OVER ──→ TO ──→ YOU ─────────────
```

Build up your family communication level by using nonverbal techniques. Here are a few ideas with tremendous possibilities.

MAKE A MOVE

Gestures offer new avenues for getting a message across to your family.

* SMILE: A smile has an amazing versatility; use it for greeting, encouraging, empathizing.
* WINK: Although often associated with romance, in families it can be used for a variety of messages from warning to encouragement.
* LOOK INTENSELY: Attention is the greatest reward one individual can offer to another. Looking closely can make the shy individual blossom.
* LAUGHING: When you laugh at family members' stories or cute remarks, you will provide a tremendous ego booster.
* CLAPPING: Clapping is so highly thought of that Italian operas employ a claque to applaud and Russians join in applauding themselves. Use clapping when someone in the family does something particularly good.
* THUMB AND FIRST FINGER IN A CIRCLE: Beats the most ornate congratulatory greeting card and has the advantage of immediate reward.

PROPINQUITY PROVIDES POSSIBILITIES

For far too long we have associated body closeness with sexual intentions. It has a much richer meaning than that. Use proximity for helping your family communication.

* WALKING AS A FAMILY: Visit a German park, woodland, or even open field on a Sunday afternoon, and you will see the whole German family dressed in Sunday best as they walk together. In our mechanized age, we may have lost the value of "going for a walk." A family out walking learns a new solidarity.
* SITTING WITH CHILDREN: Famous essayist F. W. Boreham always recollected "hassock hour" as children sat on the floor surrounding their mother seated on a hassock. Parents sitting with children provides a good experience. Some children cherish those moments when mother or father sits on the bed even though little may be said.

* EATING TOGETHER: We can eat together around the table at mealtimes or on a special visit to the Pizza Hut or the hamburger joint. Eating apparently has some special significance as a family ritual.
* PLAYING GAMES: You might paraphrase a well-known saying "the family that plays together stays together." Let's do some more about family games. Outdoor games in the summer or parlor games on a winter's night help to build a spirit of closeness with each other.

TOUCH AND GLOW

A visitor to a continental orphanage noted a fat peasant woman carrying a baby on her hip. In answer to his inquiry he was told, "That's old Anna. Whenever a baby is sickly, Anna takes it, carries it around, holding it close to her body and giving it bodily contact and affection."

* TOUCHING: In one particularly effective therapy group when a group member feels another member is needing some support or encouragement, he "reaches out"—touches, takes a hand, pats on the shoulder. If a family is to fulfill its function, touching must be an integral part of its activities.
* HUGGING: I once knew a very sedate school principal. Past middle-life, she overawed me. Seeing her after a space of time, I hugged her. Some ten years later she wrote to me recalling, of all things, "that wonderful hug." Many people need some good wholesome bodily contact.
* HOLDING ON LAP: The little girl loved a particular story. Whenever her father asked what story she wanted, she would make the same request. Becoming rather bored with the routine telling of the story, daddy recorded it on cassette and then showed the little girl how to operate the machine. Shortly afterwards she came with a request for "the story." Daddy responded, "But you have it on the cassette player." The little girl responded, "Yes, I know, but the cassette player doesn't have a lap."
* PATTING HEAD, SHOULDER, OR HAND: Martin Luther pushed through the jostling crowd at Worms as he approached the scene of his confrontation with his accusers. General Frundsberg, the most illustrious soldier of Germany, reached out and clapped him on the shoulder. Always note the encouragement the action brought to Luther. A touch may make all the difference.

Use gestures, togetherness experiences, and bodily contact to strengthen family communication.

Trouble on the Channel

As it passes from the transmitter to the receiver, the message-signal may be interfered with in a number of ways.

Trouble on the Channel

Type D Distortions Occur as a Statement Passes from One Family Member to Another

What we generally refer to as communication is the step in which the message is transmitted from the mouth through the air to the ear of the receiver. For our purpose we will refer to this link in the communication chain as the channel.

$$\text{TRANSMITTER} \longrightarrow \text{CHANNEL} \longrightarrow \text{RECEIVER}$$

This terminology opens the possibility of confusion about the words used by communication theorists. Sometimes the word *medium* is used, and some theorists go as far as to say there are many channels along which different signals travel— the auditory channel, the visual channel, and the tactile channel. We will confine ourselves to speaking of one channel along which a wide variety of types of signals may travel.

Modern communications methods utilize one channel for many different types of signals; so a company may lease one port of a satellite and beam voice messages, computer data, and television programs on that single channel. News has also come of a wire used among other things for airplane controls. It does away with sheaths of many different wires. Different signals are transmitted using what is called a "time-sharing principle," with the signals only one-millionth of a second apart. We will discuss the single channel as providing for a great variety of messages.

What has been called the most romantic enterprise in American history was launched on April 3, 1860. The Pony Express

employed such well-known personalities as Wild Bill (James
B.) Hickock and Buffalo Bill (William F.) Cody. The firm of
Russell, Majors, and Waddell, proprietors of the venture, went
to the expense of building 190 relay stations, buying 500 of the
finest horses, and recruiting over 200 riders—average age 18.
Each rider was given a Bible and strict prohibitions against
any drinking or swearing.

These daring young riders raced through the desert regions,
over sage-covered valleys and low ranges, and across the bad-
lands. As they spurred on their horses, they were attacked by
highwaymen, hostile Indians, marauding animals, and devastating blizzards. Despite all this they generally got through.

An Arab proverb says, "Language is a swift horse which conveys a man into distant lands." A message-signal traveling on
the air waves between transmitter and receiver is as much
open to predators as was the Pony Express.

As contradictory as it may seem, modern technological de-
velopments have enlarged the possibility of waylaying a
message-signal. Confronted with the Iron Curtain encircling
the Communist countries, lovers of freedom, believing in the
power of an idea, conceived Radio Liberty and Radio Free
Europe. Communist governments, on the other hand, un-
willing to let their people listen to the news of free and open
societies, responded with an enormous program of jamming
the signals from the West. It has been estimated that Moscow
uses enough electricity to light a city of one million people
for a year in its efforts to keep out the message of Radio Liberty. Thus, they waylay the message-signal as it passes along
the channel from the transmitter to the receiver to create what
emigree author Alexander Solzhenitsyn calls the "muffled
zone."

In interpersonal communications distorting techniques are
equally effective but somewhat more subtle as will be seen in
the four varieties of Type D Distortions:

Type D1: Why honey doesn't hear
Type D2: Talking down and talking up
Type D3: The use and abuse of silence
Type D4: Low booster power

5. Why Honey Doesn't Hear

*Type D1 Distortions: Failure of Husband
and Wife to
Communicate with
Each Other*

Sitting upright in the uncomfortable chair, Mrs. Dill is obviously ill at ease in the principal's office. Mr. Renfro, seated across the desk, has been through this experience many times before, but he never finds it easy. Tom, Mrs. Dill's fifteen-year-old, was caught handing over a packet of amphetamines to another student; hence this interview.

Greeting formalities completed, Mrs. Dill answers an unasked question, "Mr. Dill couldn't come; he had business out of town."

"Did you and your husband talk about the matter before he left?"

"No we didn't . . ." Mrs. Dill trails off as the tears begin to roll down her cheeks, ". . . we never talk about anything."

Mrs. Dill has summed up a fundamental difficulty of husband-wife relationships.

Next time you board a commercial aircraft and the stewardess speaks over the PA system, listen. You may learn something about the nature of communication. Notice particularly her request to read the card in the seat pocket. In addition to such frightening information as to how to get oxygen if the plane is depressurized, emergency exits in case of a crash, and the location of life belts, this little card contains a warning against using portable radio receivers. This is because some radio receivers send signals that may interfere with the plane's

navigational instruments. The receiver may also be a transmitter.

Human communications are like this. Two people communicating do not maintain fixed roles. The listener may suddenly
become a speaker, whereupon the speaker is transformed into
a listener.

Webster's dictionary gives us a clue to two ideas inherent in
the word *communication*. One definition reads, "An act or instance of transmitting," but an alternative meaning states it
as, "A process by which meanings are exchanged between individuals through a common system of symbols." Another way
of saying this is that communication is a process and proceeds,
not in a straight line, but rather in a circle.

One popular way of categorizing communication skills is to
divide them into two broad groups—expressive skills, which
include speaking and writing, and assimilative skills, listening
and reading.

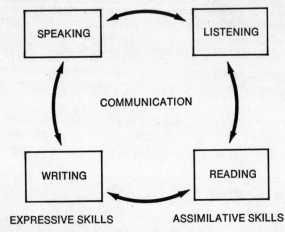

The word *organization* is used to describe the coordinated
activity of an interdependent group of people within which
both the expressive and assimilative skills of communication
are of first-rate importance. Nowhere is this truer than in the
organization we call the family.

Studies in organizational life have shown that communication takes place on three levels—downward, upward, and laterally.

Downward communication is the message-signal the executive wishes to get to the rank and file members of the organization. With the aid of public-address systems, bulletins, conferences, memos, the executive tries to get out information concerning the enterprise in which the organization is involved. Some studies have revealed a great loss in downward communication. In moving down through the organization as much as 80 percent of the material may be lost.

Upward communication takes place as members of the organization try to get their message-signal up to the higher echelons. This is the most difficult of all communication and takes a lot of work on the part of the leader to get the information from the rank and file. One authority claims a top-line executive needs to spend at least 40 percent of his time listening if he is to get the necessary feedback.

Both upward and downward communication in family life will be discussed in chapter 6.

Lateral communication describes the interchange of message-signals between two people at similar executive levels. Though they both belong to the same institution, they may build their own little empires and in the process keep information from each other. In this way they ignore both the communication and interdependency aspects of organizational life.

A similar situation exists in the family unit, but there are some distinctions which make lateral communication more critical in the family than it is in other forms of organizational life. Husband and wife are ideally a partnership. The Bible says that in marriage they have become "one flesh," a rich expression implying at least a very deep communication. They lay the foundation for all later communication in the family, and the basis they build will in a large measure determine the whole structure of communications that will later characterize that particular family unit.

Lateral communication in family life is complicated by a number of factors which bring Type D1 Distortions.

(1) *Failure to build and maintain a communication base.*

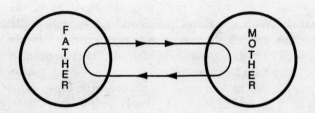

The basic communication flow of family life should be between husband and wife.

Conversation is a lost art! So say many observers of the passing scene as they contrast the spirited tête-à-tête of former years with the pathetic conversational efforts of people at a contemporary social gathering.

If you want to see how badly the conversational art has deteriorated, just peep in on a husband and wife. Go to a restaurant and look around the tables where a man and a woman are looking into each other's eyes and excitedly carrying on a spirited conversation—they're not married.

On the other hand, if they give the appearance of being a couple of strangers the maître d' has fitted in at the same table and if they are eating with a quiet earnestness and silently working their way through the meal, there's a good chance they're husband and wife. Bound by a solemn marriage vow, they are conversationally separated from each other by a great chasm.

The conversational art requires both thought and work on the part of the participants, but it's an art that once mastered will enrich a husband-wife relationship.

In many ways a conversation is like a game of tennis played by two friends who have no need to defeat each other, playing the game so they can keep the rally going. Like the tennis serve, the opening of a conversation is all important.

A conversation may be opened in one of five ways:

(1) *A greeting*—"Hi." "How are you?" "Good morning."

(2) *A request for information*—"What time does the plane leave?" "Have you been waiting long?"

(3) *An offer of information*—"Did you hear about the president's speech?" "Can I help you?" "Do you know your way?"

(4) *An expression of anger, pain, or joy*—"Wowee!" "Ouch!" "How about that?"

(5) *A substitute statement*—This type of opening remark is used in the hope of diverting a statement about to be made. The boss finds himself in the elevator with a secretary he suspects is going to ask for a raise, so he says, "It sure was raining hard this morning . . ."

Like serving the ball in tennis, the conversation opener anticipates the ball may be hit back to him. The receiver, on the other hand, must take a certain risk, for once the ball has been returned who knows where the conversation will go.

Mr. Harrison, an affluent banker from Birmingham, Alabama, traveling in the plane from New York was seated alongside a bright-looking young man. After the takeoff the young man addressed Mr. Harrison, "Could you tell me the time"?

Mr. Harrison replied, "Oh, shut up."

The young man was mollified and said, "Why did you talk to me in that way? I just asked a simple question. Why didn't you give me a civil answer?"

Mr. Harrison looked at his companion, "Well, I'll tell you why I didn't want to answer your question. If I answer your question, you'll start a conversation about the weather and politics and one thing leads to another. I notice you have a southern accent, I invite you to my house. At home you meet my daughter, you ask her for a date, then you fall in love. You come and ask me if you can marry my daughter. Why should I go to all that trouble? Let me tell you right now, I won't let my daughter marry anyone who doesn't even own a watch."

Like Mr. Harrison, many of us feel opening a conversation may make us vulnerable, but we must at all cost build a communication base for our marriage.

Once the base has been established, it must be maintained,

a practice which isn't as simple as it first sounds. A husband and wife must continue to react to each other, but in the interactional experiences there may be sensitive areas. At one extreme on the continuum there is ignoring each other, and at the other end the possibility of overreacting. One way of viewing this overreaction is to see it as the pendulum effect.

Haney,[1] who has formulated this concept, sees discussion between two people as being represented by a pendulum. No matter what might be the true facts in a discussion between two people they almost invariably see themselves as fair and objective. But once involved in the discussion they frequently become more convinced than ever that they are right and that their fellow conversationalist is offering some unreliable ideas. Then strange things begin to happen.

Mr. and Mrs. Appelton are a compatible couple and have a similar outlook in many areas, but there are times when they find themselves interacting in a way that all too easily pushes each of them into an "either/or" position. They find themselves involved in a conversation that is miles from where it started.

On the subject of the discipline of the children they are generally agreed, but you might not think so if you heard them on a certain Tuesday night. Mrs. Appelton was reporting the behavior of John Naylor while his mother and he were visiting that Friday afternoon in the Appelton house.

Mr. and Mrs. Appelton both see themselves as neutral on the discipline question.

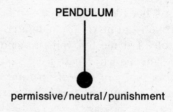

PENDULUM

permissive/neutral/punishment

MRS. APPELTON:
You just should have seen that John Naylor in action. I certainly think children should be permitted to express themselves, but I was scared he was going to push over your aquarium.

MRS. APPELTON:
That's the problem in America today. Mrs. Naylor has obviously raised her children in this permissive John Dewey idea. She should have given that kid a paddling right on the spot.

MRS. APPELTON:
Oh, you men. You always think that everything can be solved by hitting the children. You think that brute force is the answer to every situation.

MRS. APPELTON:
There you go. A good whipping never hurt anybody. All this permissive talk and that whole idea of being soft on children has raised a generation of delinquents.

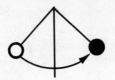

MRS. APPELTON:
That cruel attitude makes delinquents. Because of these re-
pressive attitudes we have messed up more children. Our
whole idea of crime and punishment has been to put people
into jails, and so we've made a lot more criminals.

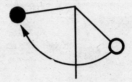

As the discussion goes on, the two of them are forced into
taking positions they really don't believe in, but they take
them in reaction to a spouse and illustrate the pendulum effect.
   Watch out for the pendulum effect! Discuss the way it
works with your spouse. When you are having a discussion,
notice the movement. If you see a situation like this develop-
ing, try to short-circuit the potentially damaging movement.
Say, for example, "Check! We're getting caught up in the
pendulum effect. I'm not going to take this extreme position.
Let me explain a number of qualifications I wish to make."
   Another conversation stopper is the put-down response.
Some of these are just space-fillers, but others give the speaker a
certain satisfaction in having made a clever response.
   Put-downs include:
   "I know I'm wasting my breath, but . . ."
   "No one in his right mind could believe that . . ."
   "Everybody knows that . . ."
   "Where did you get that goofy idea?"
   "It really isn't any of my business, but . . ."
   "Why do you always think you know more than anybody
else?"
   "If you're not interested in hearing the facts . . . okay . . ."
   "Whoever told you you could wear blue?"
   "Well, sweetie, those pants don't do a thing for you."
   "Are you trying to be funny?"
   "I don't want to hurt your feelings, but . . ."

"If I tell you something, will you promise not to get mad?"

You can have one of two attitudes toward put-downs. You can cherish the moment of ego inflation in having been smart, or you can take the long look and ask yourself if this will really strengthen your relationship and be willing to forego your ego trip by moving to a better interaction rather than derailing your conversational partner.

If you feel the interaction between you and your spouse is slowing down, why not try some conversational stimulators? These might include:

Let your spouse save face. People often make foolish statements which are obviously incorrect; you don't have to put your partner right—*keep listening.*

Be as pleasant and friendly with your husband or wife as you would with an outsider, and don't forget to *listen.*

The honest "I don't know" is often the best reply to some question about a matter in which your information is very limited—then *listen.*

People are always more interested in themselves than they are in you—*so listen.*

As your spouse talks, formulate a question that will encourage him or her and then *listen for the answer.*

Play conversational tennis, seeing how adept you can become in hitting the conversational ball back to your mate and wait for a return *by listening.*

Watch for warning signals, be sensitive to your partner's reactions. If you are not doing so well, *try listening for awhile.*

(2) *A reluctance to accept responsibility.*

This form of Type D1 Distortion complicates lateral communication as seen by the experience of the Simpsons. Billy is about normal for a healthy sixteen-year-old, fair in his academic record, a pretty good basketball player, and an enthusiastic if somewhat indifferent strummer of the guitar. But whatever he lacks in the educational, sports, or music fields, he makes up for with unbounded confidence.

He has reached the stage in life when his mind is preoccupied with automobiles. By taking a driver's education course at school, he had gained his license and now was spending a good proportion of his waking moments devising ways to get behind the wheel of the family car.

Planning his strategy carefully, he offered to help with the dishes that evening. That move itself ought to have been sufficient warning to Mrs. Simpson. Dishes finished, Billy casually mentioned that he needed a special book from the downtown library and asked his mother, "Do you think it will be okay for me to drive the car down to the library?"

Mrs. Simpson had certain questions in her mind about Billy's driving prowess, but he had been so helpful that she hated to turn him down flat. "Why don't you ask your father?"

In her mind she half-planned to get a signal to her husband, but the phone rang, and long-winded Mrs. Sensor from the PTA launched into an extended account of the plans for the annual carnival.

Billy disappeared into the den.

Mr. Simpson hardly looked up. Buried in his book, he had no burning desire to visit with his offspring.

Billy took the initiative, "I have to go down to the library, dad. I've talked to mother about it, and she says if it's all right with you I can take the car."

"Take the car." Bill Simpson had always had misgivings about his son's driving ability. Well, apparently Charlotte was satisfied; so he reached into his pocket and handed over the keys.

An hour later the phone rang.

Charlotte answered and heard Billy's distressed voice. He'd had a wreck over on the north side of the city miles away from the library. When she broke the news to her husband, Mr. Simpson blew his top and demanded to know why she had agreed to let Billy take the car.

It is better to draw a veil over the next ten minutes as George and Charlotte blamed each other for the problem.

This painful situation is an example of a Type D1 Distortion which spoils the lateral communication in the Simpson household. It need not have arisen if one of the parents had the courage to make a decision. Mrs. Simpson should have made her decision instead of leaving it to her husband. Mr. Simpson, on the other hand, easily rationalized that his wife had decided and so she was to blame.

What should we do in these situations?

Remember the importance of lateral communication within the family.

Realize you cannot go on evading responsibility by passing the decisions over to your spouse. You must accept your share of the responsibility.

It is impossible to always be popular with your children. Some decisions must be made no matter how you perceive your children's reactions toward you personally.

Deliberately set aside some time when you and your spouse are going to review what is happening in the family, what the children are doing, how these activities fit in with the total family plans.

(3) *Intervention by children.* Lateral communication in the family between husband and wife is further complicated by the activities of children who in looking out for their own survival, interests, and aspirations divide their parents.

Mrs. Banton's problems with her daughter Sheila are typical. Mrs. Banton sometimes had the impression that her eleven-year-old daughter could create more difficulties than any two children. Because she had a heavy schedule, Mrs. Banton warned Sheila to be home on the dot at 4:00 P.M. Sheila forgot the admonition and after school had gone home with her friend Joan.

Mrs. Banton was depending on Sheila to look after their two-year-old while she rushed down to the store to straighten up their account. By the time Sheila came in at 5:30, her mother was thoroughly irked and let fly with a stream of re-criminations. Then she delivered her final blow, "You just wait till your daddy hears about this. He'll give you the paddling of your life."

As soon as mother mentioned daddy's name, the situation became serious. Mr. Banton was a no-nonsense father, and once his wife got him really stirred up, he dispensed discipline with a heavy hand.

So it happened that as Mr. Banton came driving up within three blocks of his home who should flag him down but his daughter Sheila. Seldom had that daughter of his been so friendly as she told him about school work and church and finally let him know that very few friends of hers were as fortunate as she. It was so good to have a father with whom she could talk.

Sheila snuggled up to her daddy, "All the girls say that I've got such a wonderful daddy, that I'm the luckiest girl."

Small wonder that when Mrs. Banton tried to tell her spouse about Sheila's earlier irresponsible behavior, she found him only half listening and pointing out that you can't put an old head on young shoulders. Surely she remembered that when she was a girl she didn't have a good sense of time.

Communicating with the children requires a special skill, especially when it has to do with decision making. Here are some special considerations.

Make sure you understand the children's proposition. Get all the information. They are probably telling the truth, but even the truth looks different when you know the whole story.

Don't talk to each other through the children. You can discuss it in their presence, spelling out the pros and cons, or you can insist on the right to talk together and then announce your decision and perhaps the reasons for it. But make sure you have a face-to-face conversation with your spouse.

Don't be stampeded into a hasty decision. Take your time. Things are seldom as urgent as children make them out to be.

If discipline is to be administered, it should be done immediately. Don't hold judgment over the heads of the children by threatening, "Wait until your father comes home." There is a good chance he won't enjoy being used as a policeman.

Keep a united front. Even if your spouse is making a mistake and you feel tempted to correct him or her, don't do it. Don't interfere. Perhaps afterward you can discuss the wisdom of the action, but don't do it in front of the children.

While Julius Caesar may have devised the strategy of dividing to conquer in warfare, children have perfected the technique in controlling their parents.

A man and his wife had come to the counseling center to consult about a problem with their adolescent son. While the wife talked on rapidly, the husband sat quietly by until she said, "My husband has a communication problem with our son."

The husband testily responded, "I don't have a communication problem *with him*; he has a communication problem *with me*. I communicate plenty, but he just sits there without saying a word."

Although he obviously didn't realize it, the father certainly had a communication problem on his hands. Communication is never a one-way process, and the father had failed to recognize the circular nature of communication.

As far as I know, Thor Hyerdahl had no interest in assimilative communication skills, but if he and other scientists had developed as much concern with feedback as with scientific research, it would have saved the scientific fraternity a lot of time and labor.

This unusual scientist concentrated on the mysteries of human migration and had floated across the Pacific on a balsa raft known as a *kon tiki*. While on this Pacific jaunt he developed an interest in Easter Island, also somewhat anthropologically referred to as the "navel of the world."

As the third scientific expedition to the island, Heyerdahl's party tried to grapple with many of its mysteries. None puzzled them more than the enormous statues as tall as houses and heavy as box cars that lay strewn around. However on earth did people in this primitive culture with no engineering techniques manage to raise and position these tremendous hunks of carved stone?

The mayor of the island, Don Pedro, was a somewhat talkative individual, and Heyerdahl had questions about his credibility. When asked how the statues moved from one part of the island to the other, the mayor often smiled and said they walked.

One day out of the clear blue sky Heyerdahl popped a question to the mayor: "Don't you know how these giants were raised?"

"Yes, senor, I know. There's nothing to it."

Somewhat skeptical that this might be more native bragga-docio, Heyerdahl proceeded to query him, but the mayor continued stoutly to maintain that he could raise a statue himself providing he had enough help.

So Heyerdahl commissioned him to do just that.

Employing the services of a large group of fellow citizens, the mayor obtained three long wooden poles which they used as levers. As they combined their efforts on the poles, they raised the head of the statue a fraction of an inch. Helpers, sprawled on the ground, pushed stones under it.

They continued the process, alternately levering and push-ing more stones, gradually building up the stone supports. Finally they had the statue standing upright.

Scarcely daring to believe his own eyes, the researcher turned on the mayor and reminded him of all the investigators who had tried to discover the secret of how the statues were erected. He asked, "Why didn't you tell all these people?"

The mayor responded, "No one asked me."

There are many family members who know a lot more than we give them credit for. If we listen to them for feedback, we may be agreeably surprised.

```
_____ OVER ——→ TO ——→ YOU _____
```

UPGRADING HUSBAND-WIFE COMMUNICATION

(1) Why not have a regular "State of the Union"—"Marriage Union," that is—session for you and your spouse?

(2) Decide on a place. Somewhere you can be private—no children present—no television or other distractions.

(3) Choose a time. You may have to go for a shorter period at first— say 8:00 to 8:30 P.M.

(4) Set up ground rules—a series of "no-no's."

　* No attempts to go back over the past history—keep all the discussion in the present—"here and now."

　* No "zaps." Zaps are insulting statements that husband and wives make to each other.

　　　Harry: "You certainly are a nagger." Pat replies:

　　　"That's a zap." Harry apologizes.

　* No blaming. Realize a married person has a built-in alibi. A spouse is available for blame. This must be cut away. Each agrees to focus on his or her own behavior in the relationship.

　* No interrupting. Let your mate have a fair say.

　* No threats or ultimatums.

(5) Get underway. If the situation is badly deteriorated you may need to decide on equal time. Ten minutes for her and ten for him— ten to try and reach a compromise.

(6) Don't be discouraged if your first session is not very successful— keep on.

6. Talking Down and Talking Up

Type D2 Distortions: *A Frustration of Communication from Children to Parents or Parents to Children*

The group of women sat around the darkened room in a state of expectancy. They had gathered for a seance, and the medium addressed them, "Is there any loved one who has passed on with whom you would like to make contact?"

Mrs. Meeves quickly responded, "Never mind about those in the hereafter. Can you help me communicate with my teenage son?"

A conscientious father laments, "I can't talk with my kids; they don't hear me."

A frustrated teenager declares, "Mom and dad don't understand me." All of this occurs within a family, the group relationship that should provide the most meaningful of all communication experiences.

Any group of people can provide insights into the theory and practice of communication, but few do it more clearly than a therapy group in which interpersonal communications are constantly under consideration and evaluation. This was dramatized for me as I worked with a group of drug addicts moving toward discharge from hospital and a new way of life.

Every session brought its quota of surprises as I was initiated into the language, life, and peculiar thinking of the drug culture. Then came a heated discussion that climaxed in a group member's throwing down the gauntlet as he addressed himself to me and the chaplain, "It's us against you."

I had stumbled upon the we-they phenomenon, sometimes referred to as "the code of the streets," based upon the commandment, "Thou shalt not squeal." This attitude sees the whole of society as divided between the establishment and the criminal, a division and a dichotomy that is the bane of law enforcement people.

The same principle emerges in family life where the children often speak about their parents using the impersonal *they*. "*They* won't let me go with you for the weekend." "*They* won't let me have the automobile." "*They* want me to be in by midnight." This we-they dichotomy is responsible for many of the problems we see in family life today.

We have already noted the importance of lateral communication that keeps parents in tune with each other, but a family is an interacting unit which involves the vertical as well as the horizontal dimension. Parents cannot afford to be a shoulder-to-shoulder unit resisting all the encroachments of the other family members. The vertical dimension of communication is crucial to the development of good effective family experiences.

The basic communication pattern is between parents. Then as children grow and develop, they become an increasingly meaningful part of the communication pattern of the interacting family unit. All too frequently children's growth and development means that while they communicate vigorously with their peers they lose interest in vertical communication with their parents.

We must bend every effort to the task of building vertical family communications, and this may begin with downward communication as parents hone their skills in getting their message across to their family unit.

Downward Communication

One vivid memory of boyhood days was my chore of running errands to the store. My Australian mother referred to these as "messages," and in many ways the message was the heart of the process. As a small lad I was given to dreaming and was

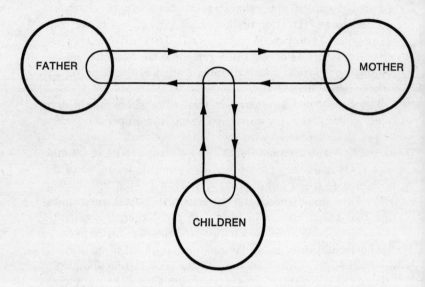

Communication proceeds in a number of different directions in a family
unit. While it is fundamental that parents must communicate with
each other, it is equally important there be vertical communication
between the parents and the children and the children and the parents.

easily diverted from my task by the side attractions I encountered as I made the rounds from home to store and back again.

My mother adopted a time-honored technique. She wrote
out the "'message" on a piece of paper, carefully wrapped the
money in it, placed it all in an envelope, and then with a long
safety pin affixed the whole thing inside my shirt pocket.

That parent of mine had hit upon what management special-
ist Charles E. Redfeld has concluded about the business world,
"The written word is not distortion proof, but it suffers less
from distortion over a period of time or in a lengthy channel
than does its oral counterpart."

This may give us a clue to downward communication with
our children. We must have clear understandings about our
expectations from our offspring. We need to establish the
boundaries within which they function. Workers in the field
of behavior modification are teaching parents how to establish

some sort of order in their relationships to their children. Every member of the family has some responsibility; consequently, rules of family life become a necessity. The following guidelines may help you in establishing some rules.

(1) Don't be frightened to make contracts with your children; put them down in black and white so that everybody understands just what it's all about.

(2) State in as few words as possible what behavior is desired, but don't let brevity keep you from specifying necessary details. Don't write, "Jimmy will be a good boy," but "Jimmy will help with the dishes," or "Joe will mow the lawn each Friday," or "Pat will be home from school by 4:15." Have the contractual arrangement written down and displayed in the proper place.

(3) Make clear the consequence of desired behavior. Use the "If-Then" principle: "If you do your homework, you can watch TV"; "If you come home on time, you will be able to go out later."

(4) Be careful to state the rule so it is clear if it has been violated.

(5) When there is a violation, have the child repeat the rule so that he or she understands exactly what happened.

(6) Don't formulate a rule unless it is necessary, and after it works successfully, fade it out.

Written agreements will provide a basis for understanding by both children and parents as to what parents expect of their children.

Written messages may have an even wider application and may help with horizontal as well as vertical communication. One marriage counselor provides a husband and wife with thirty cards apiece; fifteen of the cards are white and fifteen yellow. Whenever a spouse does something pleasing, his or her mate writes it down on a white card; an unpleasing act is written on a yellow card. They are instructed to describe the behavior specifically . For example, a wife should not write, "You put me down when we had friends," but "When Mary Jo asked me about the new supermarket, you said, 'She doesn't know anything about shopping.'"

This system has a number of advantages. A husband and wife don't stew over things but write them down immediately. Thus they short-circuit the process whereby an idea continues to fester and grow. When they exchange cards later, they have a basis for discussion. They also have a record they can use to count up behaviors and list the things they need to learn. Best of all, some people learn for the first time to become aware of some of their spouse's good points. They had long been vaguely aware of these but had never been specific or told the spouse, and they are surprised and overjoyed to see the result when they share it with their partner.

In communications, as Bacon has said it, "Writing maketh an exact man."

Offering Criticism

So much in life depends on your perspective. I do a lot of speaking at meetings and across the years have discovered that nothing raises my hackles more rapidly than watching an ineffectual ushering job. I sit up on the platform where I have a panoramic view, and from my vantage point I see the ushers cramming people into the packed back seats and leaving a great open no man's land of empty seats in front.

I sometimes tease the ushers, and occasionally one will respond, "Why don't you do it yourself?"

Although I imply I would easily do a better job in handcuffs with both legs tied together, I know that if I tried I would probably have little more success.

Most of us believe in constructive criticism, but the way we interpret this phrase depends upon our perspective. If you are offering criticism, you are aware of your altruistic ideals and the way in which you may be able to help another person develop his potential. The word *constructive* is preeminent in your mind.

However, if you are on the receiving end, the word *criticism* leaps out at you in letters of fire and your self-love is offended. You see your critic as a self-righteous individual who never looks at himself but who, from his ivory tower of self-satisfaction, spends his time searching out the faults of others. You are immediately beset with the temptation to make a reflex response by reversing the situation and criticizing him rather than fairly evaluating what has been suggested to you.

Yet criticism must be given. Coaching any sport, teaching any skill, training in any area is dependent upon some type of criticism by an onlooker. Learn the skill of tactfully offering criticism, and you can count it a major achievement.

Sugar-coat the pill of criticism. Unlike the tennis player who is paying ten dollars per hour and is most grateful for the suggestions the coach makes to him, most people feel that criticism is a blow to their self-love. Because praise is the greatest reward we can give another person, the best way to criticize is by offering praise first. In *Julius Caesar*, Shakespeare depicts Mark Antony as a man vividly aware of the importance of praise before criticism. He's out to get Brutus's scalp. Nevertheless, he leads off by saying,

> For Brutus is an honorable man;
> So are they all, all honorable men.

As he moves along, this clever speaker is able to turn tables on his enemies, arouse the mob, and achieve his original purpose.

Suppose you are worried about your wife's lack of punctuality and felt the time has come to say something. However, you are concerned because your spouse frequently interprets your efforts to pass on information as "attacking" her. How do you go about this?

You could lead off with, "Honey, I want you to know how much I appreciate the way you keep house. I'm always proud when we have guests. I'm grateful for the way you work your fingers to the bone looking after the children and for your sweet spirit in all that you do. It may be I'm a bit finicky about things, but I would sure appreciate it if you could be ready when it's time for us to leave. It bugs me when I'm late."

You have gotten your message across to your wife, but you've put a nice sugar-coating on it by paying her a series of compliments and acknowledging that you might be a little finicky.

Begin with yourself. One of the main benefits of participating in group therapy is the process of *feedback*. In such a situation the other members tell a person about some aspects of his personality that could be improved.

As practical as this procedure would appear to be, in actual practice there are some problems. It depends mainly on the way in which the criticizer goes about his work.

In our counseling center we use a type of group therapy as Integrity Therapy. The leaders have developed a way of dealing with the problem of criticism. A group member is told, "If you wish to tell someone else what to do in a given situation, you must 'earn the right' by talking about your own failures before telling anyone else about his failures."

We have discovered that when this technique is used few people are ever upset by someone in the group "putting them right." Once the person has spoken of his own failures, he establishes his position as an equal rather than a superior. From this perspective, his criticism is acceptable.

In a counseling interview Mrs. Nordan told me a moving story of communication problems with her eighteen-year-old daughter. Julia, in college, was "goofing off" and failing in her courses. She called her mother and confessed that she had been missing classes and would shortly be in difficulty with the university authorities.

Mrs. Nordan, a well-dressed, attractive matron of middle years, in her frustration asked, "What can I do?"

I asked had she as an adolescent ever "goofed off." The troubled mother sat and thought, then responded, "I certainly did. Do I have to tell you?"

"No. Not me. Why not try telling your daughter?"

Mrs. Nordan had always started discussions with her daughter by saying, "When I was a girl I . . ." and then proceeded to tell Julia about her industry and diligence, providing a list of mother's adolescent virtues. She approached Julia from her strengths! I suggested she reverse her procedure and tell Julia about her own failures in adolescence.

When Mrs. Nordan returned, she came with a smiling face. After telling Julia about her adolescent failures, her daughter had broken down to talk of her irresponsibilities and indiscretions that were complicating her life.

"Begin with yourself" might well be the motto of any successful critic.

Give your subject a chance to save his face. If the aim of criticism is to help the individual to change some facet of his life, it is a good idea to give him an out.

A friend of mine is a professor who has large classes of students in a required introductory course. Many of the students are not overly enthusiastic, and some use the time in class to catch up on their reading for other courses.

From his elevated platform the professor can see far more than the students ever imagine. When he sees a student reading, it bugs him no end, but he has learned to maintain a calm outward appearance.

The professor addresses his class, "I may be wrong, but I've got an idea that a student is reading a book that has no connection with this course. As I said, I may be mistaken, but if it is the case, I will certainly have it in mind when I prepare the grades for the members of this class."

The professor has served a notice of warning on the transgressor who generally manages to do something about the situation. Nevertheless, this professor has also provided the individual with an out by saying, "I may be mistaken."

Statements like, "I could be wrong," "Perhaps I am looking at it the wrong way," "I may not have made the situation clear at the beginning," "Perhaps I should have explained things and not left it open for misinterpretation," all help to provide the individual with a way by which he can change and not feel too badly about it.

Issue a courteous challenge. There are times when someone

in your family must be told to change a procedure, and there is very little to commend and not much sense in the critic speaking of his own failure.

A pastor of a large church had managed to persuade his congregation to buy time on television. Wanting to make maximum use of this video time, he sought the aid of a television consultant. The expert suggested they present their program in its normal format. After the presentation the consultant spoke to the minister of music who had planned and performed on the program. The consultant said, "Are you thin-skinned? Can you take criticism?"

The minister of music replied that he wanted help from the expert. Whereupon the visitor said, "I don't think you ought to sing solos on television."

How I wish this courageous man would talk with some singers I know. Think of how much suffering many of us would be saved.

The secret lay in the challenge, "Are you thin-skinned? Can you take criticism?"

In the give and take of the communication process, few areas will ever be as difficult as giving criticism, but few will have as much possibility for helping other people achieve their potential.

Upward Communication

On many television programs the late news is preceded by the question, "Do you know where your children are?" Rather unfortunately, although many parents know their children's physical location, there's a good chance they might not have any knowledge as to where they really are in any other sense because vertical communication is minimal.

What are our children thinking and saying? As a father I have always wanted to use some of my professional techniques and say, "Okay, kids, take a piece of paper and pencil. True or False?" and proceed with this quiz to discover what they are thinking. Although I can do this with my students, I realize it's more difficult with my children.

We must start early in life with them and inaugurate a program that will help our family develop vertical communication skills.

What is the most important factor in determining a child's philosophy of life? Church? Public school? Parents' religious beliefs?

None of these if we believe Ernest Ligon who once claimed the most important single factor in determining a child's philosophy was what was talked about at the dinner table. It certainly is the place for developing family communication. Some social scientists claim the only time a family ever has a face-to-face confrontation is when they sit down to eat a meal. This occasion provides an unusual opportunity for developing communication skills.

The Fowler family has really worked at this. The meal commences with a family ritual—a most important factor in developing family solidarity—as they hold hands and give thanks for the food. Henry Fowler, the father, often voices the prayer, sometimes it's one of the children, and on other occasions they all join together in singing the blessing.

Once the meal is under way, Lynn Fowler will frequently say, "Well, let's find out what happened today. Jim, you lead off. How went your day?" and so on around the table.

Humor plays its part. Henry will ask, "Did anyone hear a funny story today?"

The stories are sometimes rather haltingly told, but everybody stays "on task," listens, and at the conclusion Mr. and Mrs. Fowler find something to commend about the storytelling.

On occasions the Fowlers form themselves into a family council. In this council the children are asked to express themselves on some of the issues that confront the family. "Where will we go for our vacation this year?" "How about this proposed new car—any ideas?" "Should we take a family trip to Six Flags?"

Mr. and Mrs. Fowler have also promoted the "conference" idea. Any child who wishes can ask for a conference with either or both parents. He or she has a ten-minute period of time thus coming to feel what he or she has to say is of importance to both father and mother.

The conference plan indicates the Fowlers are concerned with vertical aspects of communication.

Vertical communication within a family may encounter its stiffest resistance as the children enter adolescence. Children who were formerly open and communicative all too frequently become secretive and build a wall between themselves and the other members of the family. One father of a four-year-old bothered by the constant prattle of his child commented: "Talk! Talk! Talk! Thank heavens, in a few years he'll be a teenager and we won't be able to communicate with him!"

But when these adolescent years come, a parent faced with incommunicado teenagers may have some troubled moments. A father sitting at home and watching the technological miracle of pictures and sound beamed millions of miles from the moon to the earth, mentally contrasts this communications feat with his difficulty of getting a message across the living room to his son Jimmy.

The adolescent greatly resembles a beginning water skier. Anyone can water ski. It is one of the simplest skills to learn. Children of five and six become competent skiers. One man mastered the skill on the day of his seventy-fifth birthday.

Despite all this, one simple aspect of the process keeps many people from enjoying the sensation of skimming on the surface of the water. It is the problem of getting up and out of the water.

Most people fail because they try too hard. Instead of letting the boat pull them up, the would-be skier struggles to pull himself out of the water. Then wham! The skis fly out from under him, and he topples over to disappear below the surface. If the area of water below the surface represents childhood, and the surface of the water adulthood, then adolescence is that horrible period of coming up out of the water. Like the skiing dropout, the adolescent wants to be up on top, skimming around, enjoying all the privileges of adulthood, but he tries too hard and often falls flat on his face.

The parent anxiously watching a stumbling adolescent is mollified when the advice offered from years of adult experience is summarily rejected. If this impasse is to be overcome, we must develop a technique of communication, and one of the most effective might be the process of negotiation.

For a long time the negotiation-communication technique has been used in situations where differences exist—international diplomacy, labor-management disputes, ethnic or religious controversies. The principle has already been applied to some of the problems of parent-child relationships. The marriage counselor is in many senses an arbitrator; family courts do the same thing; and the psychologist has long found himself as the mediator of the generations. More recently psychotherapy has developed family therapy which involves mediation.

The following principles may help in the negotiating process:

Maintain your self-control. Much talk by your teenager will sound unreasonable if not downright impertinent, but make some allowances for the brashness of immature youth. If he loses his temper, you descend to his level if you lose yours.

Be prepared to acknowledge your own failures. One father shouted, "I'm right. Even when I'm wrong, I'm right."

We adults make plenty of mistakes. If we acknowledge them, our teenager is often ready for dialogue.

One father who had been particularly rough on his son said, "Jim, I was wrong. I shouldn't have lost my temper. I'm sorry."

The boy responded, "I shouldn't have taken the car without asking."

Some situations are not negotiable. We can't negotiate whether or not to obey the law. The teenager must do this. This is a painful but a necessary boundary that must be set up.

Take time to listen. Remember how much your teenager glorifies communication. He's often convinced he's been on the receiving end for a long time. Now he feels his time has come.

Fight back every impulse to interrupt. Listen, listen, listen.

Just give a response of "Oh," "I see," "You sure have a point there." You may be surprised at the way in which he will talk himself out of some of the ideas that he previously held.

Acknowledge his ability to reason. When he asks why, it isn't enough simply to say, "Because I say so." Don't downgrade his weak arguments or make sarcastic comments. Use good-natured questions that will help him face his own inconsistencies. Ask him about his recommendations.

Start a new train of thought. Say, "Have you thought of this?" "What will you do if this arises?" Sometimes an anecdote will help, "I once knew a fellow . . ." Reference to a newspaper cartoon or story may help to show that the problem you two are facing is part of the universal human dilemma.

Attack the act, not the person. When junior does something foolish, don't say, "You're so stupid; that's not the way to go about things."

The better way would be, "I love and respect you, but I think that action was wrong, wrong, wrong. Nevertheless, I love you, even if I don't like what you're doing."

Learn to negotiate with your adolescents. It will call for patience and understanding, but it will pay off in the long run.

Vertical communication presents problems in all types of organizations. Even such an entity as the United States Army, with its highly developed technological communication skills, has had to face some vertical communication problems as it struggled with getting a message through all levels of the chain of command. The following tongue-in-cheek report in an army communication illustrates the problem.

One day the battalion commander issued the following order to his executive officer:

"Tomorrow evening, at approximately 2000 hours, Halley's Comet will be visible in this area, an event which occurs only once every seventy-five years. Have the men fall out in the battalion area in fatigues, and I will explain this rare phenomenon to them. In case of rain, we will not be able to see anything, so assemble the men in the theater and I will show them films of it."

The executive officer related the order to the adjutant:

"By order of the colonel, tomorrow at 2000 hours Halley's Comet will appear above the battalion area. If it rains, fall the men out in fatigues, then march them to the theater where this rare phenomenon will take place, something which occurs only once every seventy-five years."

The adjutant related the order to the company commander:

"By order of the colonel, in fatigues at 2000 hours tomorrow evening, the phenomenal Halley's Comet will appear in the theater. In case of rain in the battalion area, the colonel will give another order, something which occurs once every seventy-five years."

The company commander passed the directive on to the first sergeant:

"Tomorrow at 2000 hours, the colonel will appear in the theater with Halley's Comet, something which happens every seventy-five years. If it rains, the colonel will order the comet into the battalion area."

The top sergeant's announcement in the formation next morning:

"When it rains tomorrow at 2000 hours, the phenomenal seventy-five-year-old General Halley, accompanied by the colonel, will drive his Comet through the battalion theater in fatigues."

If the army with all the modern means of dispensing information at its disposal faces these obstacles of vertical communication, it is small wonder that parents have problems in getting information down to the children or that offspring experience difficulty in passing on their ideas to their parents.

OVER ⟶ TO ⟶ YOU

In your dealings with your children, why not use communication as a means of changing undesirable behavior?

1. LEARN TO PINPOINT: Describe the behavior. The principle here is, "Focus on the behavior rather than the whole person."

> Not—"Please be in at a decent hour."
>
> But—"I want you to be home by 11:00 P.M.

Practice pinpointing so you will be able to use behavioral terms when you talk to your children.

2. REMEMBER TO REWARD: Attention is the greatest reward you can offer. Your communication skill comes from paying attention to and describing desirable behavior.

> Not—"Jimmy was a polite boy."
>
> But—"Did you notice the way Jimmy sat and listened without interrupting?"
>
> Not—"You are a fine lad."
>
> But—"You swept the patio beautifully."
>
> Not—"Good boy."
>
> But—"You arrived from school right on the button. You're a good guy."
>
> Not—"Fine."
>
> But—"You've done a marvelous job in getting your homework completed."

3. THE TIME SEQUENCE: Communicate your commendation the moment the desirable action takes place. Don't save up your compliments. They are not nearly as effective as if offered at the time of performance. The principle is, "Rewards have their greatest effect if given immediately on performance of the desirable behavior."

4. PUNISH WITH SUBTLETY AND FINESSE: Attention is the greatest reward, and failure to pay attention is the greatest punishment. This gives us a clue to reducing undesirable behaviors—ignore them. If a child misbehaves grossly, try T.O.—time out. Put the child in an unrewarding atmosphere—the bathroom (not his room where he has things to play with) for, say, three minutes. This practice can be very effective.

Hone up your communication skills with your family, and you will have a well-behaved and happier family unit.

7. Uses and Abuses of Silence

*Type D3 Distortions: Interference in Family
Communication by
Noise or Silence*

Mrs. Julia Harris, thirty-five years old and the mother of three, wants to enlist her husband's assistance in handling Jimmy who has been performing poorly in school.

Julia commences, "Honey, I think we should do something about Jimmy, he's . . ."

At this moment Adrian Cox, a twenty-year-old who lives at the end of the street, roars by the Harris household on his motorcycle and temporarily drowns out all conversation with a roaring staccato of ear-shattering sound.

Mr. Harris wanders off to the basement to work on a new cabinet, and when his wife finishes off the pie she's been struggling with and heads to the workshop, she hears the ringing noise of the power saw. She knows she will have to wait till later and get the television turned down so they can struggle with Jimmy's academic problems.

When Mr. Harris is finally motivated to face Jimmy, he enters his offspring's room to face another noise pollution device in the form of the stereo. It is turned up so high it seems as if Jimmy is determined to entertain Maurice Carter who lives at the other end of the block.

Noise pollution has not only become a national hazard, it has entered the front door of our homes and adds another menace to family communication.

A movie made some years ago told the story of the English people awaiting news of the outcome of the Battle of Waterloo. At this period of history the means of communication was a series of signal stations on either side of the English Channel. The anxious watchers on British soil received the message, "Wellington defeated . . . ," then fog roiled up the channel cutting off visual contact.

This distorted news threw the London business world into a state of panic. Only later when the fog cleared away was the remainder of the message received. It turned out to be, "Wellington defeated Napolean at Waterloo," which gave the whole thing an entirely different complexion. The incident of the fog cutting off communication contact is an illustration of a Type D3 Distortion.

Natural hazards often beset communication efforts. Apparently the U.S. Post Office is vividly aware of its potentialities and has taken as its motto the statement of the Greek historian Herodotus: "Neither snow nor rain nor heat nor gloom of night stays these couriers from the swift completion of their appointed routes." Many a postal patron may raise an eyebrow as he mentally compares the somewhat less than impressive performance of the postal service with its lofty statement of purpose. But the motto indicates at least some of the natural hazards that bearers of messages have encountered across the centuries.

It has remained for this present day to bring some of the most threatening challenges to effective communication in the form of noise pollution. A philosopher said, "The amount of noise which anyone can bear undisturbed stands in inverse proportion to his mental capacity and may therefore be regarded as a pretty fair measure of it."

If this statement be true, we must be in grave danger of becoming a nation of half-wits, morons, nitwits, and nincompoops, for never in our history have our delicate ears been assaulted with such a cacophony of deafening noise. We are victims of what has been called the auditory insult.

The unit most commonly used to measure sound is the decibel, named in honor of Alexander Graham Bell, famed inventor of the telephone. A decibel is defined as the faintest sound heard by the human ear. A steady noise of eighty-five decibels is considered safe, but the scale is logarithmic. An increase of ten decibels means a tenfold increase in sound intensity; twenty decibels, a hundredfold; and thirty decibels,

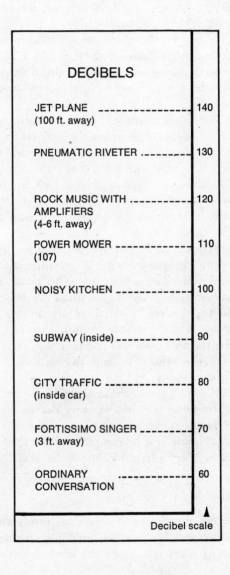

DECIBELS

JET PLANE _ _ _ _ _ _ _ _ _ _ _ _ _ _ _ _ (100 ft. away)	140
PNEUMATIC RIVETER . _ _ _ _ _ _ _ _ _	130
ROCK MUSIC WITH _ _ _ _ _ _ _ _ _ _ _ AMPLIFIERS (4-6 ft. away)	120
POWER MOWER _ _ _ _ _ _ _ _ _ _ _ _ _ (107)	110
NOISY KITCHEN _ _ _ _ _ _ _ _ _ _ _ _ _	100
SUBWAY (inside) _ _ _ _ _ _ _ _ _ _ _ _	90
CITY TRAFFIC _ _ _ _ _ _ _ _ _ _ _ _ _ _ (inside car)	80
FORTISSIMO SINGER _ _ _ _ _ _ _ _ _ (3 ft. away)	70
ORDINARY _ _ _ _ _ _ _ _ _ _ _ _ CONVERSATION	60

▲
Decibel scale

a thousandfold increase. The nature of the scale gives rise to the fallacy that if eighty-five decibels is safe, then a person needn't worry about a slight increase to eighty-six or eighty-seven decibels—"After all this is only an increase of one or two decibels." This is faulty reasoning.

As will be seen by the chart, we are victims of a noise attack wherever we go. Driving through the city, the level is eighty decibels, passing the airport at the time of the jet aircraft takeoff the intensity reaches an incredible one hundred forty decibels.

The U.S. Army has published a series of warnings to military personnel, cautioning them about the dangers to their ears of the noises they would encounter in the course of their army service. For example, troops are warned about a six-thousand-pound fork lift, a five-thousand-pound dump truck, and a Huey helicopter; yet the noise of each of these is exceeded by the noise engendered by implements encountered in a normal household.

A man may flee to the shelter of his home only to meet junior mowing the lawn with a machine giving off one hundred seven decibels of sound. The noise level in the kitchen may be as high as one hundred decibels. Everywhere he looks in the modern home there are noise-generating devices—blender, washer, dryer, vacuum cleaner, hair dryer—all polluting the air of the family domicile.

Add to these radio, TV, and stereo, and you have the ultimate in cacophony, and it's getting worse all the time. A recent report out of Austin, Texas claims overall loudness of environmental noise is doubling every decade.

William James spoke about the age in which he lived as being a megaphonic era; by comparison today, such a description would be the understatement of the year.

Creative Silence

Because communication is more than words and has to do with attitudes and feelings, we suddenly discover the paradoxical situation referred to by the famous psychiatrist Reik, who said of a psychoanalytic session, ". . . what is spoken is not the important thing. It seems to us more important to recognize what speech conceals and what silence reveals." Reik himself has written a book on psychotherapy entitled *Listening with the Third Ear*, and most trainers of psychotherapists are vividly aware that teaching the aspiring psychotherapist to keep silent is one of the most difficult tasks they face.

A troubled man went to visit his physician with a list of anxieties and fears. The wise doctor told his patient to take a day off work and visit the beach. In his hand he placed an envelope and told the man to open it when he reached his destination.

Arriving at the beach he found a quiet spot and opened the envelope. On a small piece of paper he read, "Listen carefully." Recounting the experience later, he told what a rewarding day it was. For the first time in years he heard the lapping of the waves, the song of the bird, and the sighing of the wind. Then he remembered a statement from Carlyle: "Silence is the element in which great things fashion themselves." He discovered the moment of silence could be the moment of revelation.

All this may give us a clue as to the way we can use creative silence to help others. People who master the technique of creative silence say in effect, "I could fill up the time with small talk, and there may even be something I could say which would interest you. But this is not my purpose. I want to provide you with a situation in which you can think about yourself, your failures and shortcomings, problems, assets, and future plans. Because of my interest in you, I am willing to sit in silence with you."

Like any other creative activity, this type of silence calls for self-control and diligent practice. For most of us ten seconds of silence seems like ten hours of time. The garrulous age in which we live has made us fearful of quietude. Life is too much a carnival of noise when we may really need a chapel of silence.

The Misuse of Silence

Unfortunately, even in silence the communication process can be distorted in a number of different ways, and silence can give off some strange messages.

The late Senator Thomas J. Dodd claimed that at a meeting of the politburo, Russian Kruschev ended a long tirade against the West by turning on Deputy Premier A. I. Mikoyan. "What right have you to argue with me?" Kruschev demanded.

"I never said a word," Mikoyan protested.

"Never mind, you were listening in a very aggressive manner."

Kruschev's response had some paranoid overtones, but he was correct when he implied silence carried a message. It can be defiant, rebuking, enigmatic, or punishing.

If, by some chance, you imagine silence is passive, just wait until you encounter *defiant silence*. It fairly shouts and communicates the idea, "Okay, I am going to listen. Trot out your evidence. Let's hear if you can really tell me something." Answering defiant silence is like trying to recapture an escaped parakeet in a darkened room. The responder hardly knows where to go or what to do, with his subject determined to side-step and keep him in a blind stumble.

The *silence of rebuke* is used effectively by a speaker I know who regularly addresses teenagers and is bothered when a couple of them start whispering to each other. As they commence to confer, he stops. A deathly silence follows. People being to look uncomfortable. Gradually the culprits understand, put innocent smiles on their faces, and gaze intently at the speaker. He takes up his talk again, having gained their attention with the silence of rebuke.

Enigmatic silence is rather like a person who refuses to answer a ringing phone. To respond will be to take a position, so the listener just refuses to make any response. Obstensibly, Mr. Philips is sitting listening to Mike Dorms who wants to know what the boss thinks about his new plan for reorganizing the department. As Mike excitedly presents his plan, Mr.

Philips has a faraway look in his eye. No matter how many opportunities Mike gives him to make a response, he sits like a Sphinx.

That night at home Mr. Philips explains to his wife, "Young Mike Dorms came rushing into the office with this new plan of his. I didn't let on how I felt. I know how he feels about it all, but he hasn't got any idea what I really think about the plan so I've got the drop on him."

Mrs. Philips ponders for awhile and says, "You have certainly developed these techniques, honey. I can think of three times last week when I asked you questions you never answered."

Punishing Silence

The old adage says, "Silence is golden," but for James Pelosi it was horror. A cadet at the tradition-encrusted West Point Academy, Pelosi had been accused of cheating on an engineering exam. In the trial that followed before the West Point Honor Committee, despite Pelosi's insistence on innocence and in the face of conflicting evidence, the committee convicted him. However, after reviewing the case, on the basis of the undue influence of the committee adviser, the superintendent of the academy overthrew the charge.

But it hadn't ended here. The student body of West Point had a distinctive way of handling cadets they feel to be guilty of a breach of academy honor. It is called "silencing."

Pelosi was compelled to live by himself in a room generally occupied by three. Each day he ate his meal in lonely silence at a table with places for ten, and in public he was ignored by his fellow students.

During the nineteen-month period, the ostracized cadet lost twenty-six pounds. After his graduation he remarked to a reporter, "I've taken a psychology course, and I know what isolation does to animals. No one at the academy asks how it affects a person."

Though the academy psychologist might not have specifically studied the effects of isolation on humans, the academy cadets have for a long time been aware of the effect of isolation in punishing people.

Many family members are past masters of the art of "silencing," but this skill has come to be called by such names as "pouting" and "sulking." These mechanisms are ways of using nonverbal communication as a means of attack on some fellow family member.

The word *sulky* has some interesting background. It comes primarily from the name of a vehicle, a sulky, which is described in the dictionary as "a light two-wheeled vehicle accommodating one person and drawn by one horse." From this use as a noun, the word has come to be used as an adjective, the adjective sulky being defined as "sullenly aloof, or withdrawn, gloomy, dismal."

Sulking is frequently a mechanism of control or punishment in family life.

A husband whose wife did not renew his magazine subscription lapses into silence and refuses to talk to any members of the family.

The daughter who wants to go on a trip and is not given permission retires to her room and will only answer in monosyllables when spoken to.

The child whose grandparents are visiting her home has not been allowed to go out and play so she will not talk to *anyone,* particularly the devoted grandparents.

What goes on in sulking?

It is a method of using nonverbal communication to get across a negative message. The sulker hopes that by saying nothing his message of disapproval will be projected to the person he is seeking to punish. As George Bernard Shaw said, "Silence is the most perfect expression of scorn."

Like the sulky, the word originally referred to, the sulking individual completely isolates himself and cuts himself off from other people.

The cyclical effect means the feeling of self-pity deepens and further separates the sulker from other people.

What should we do to break out of the sulking cycle?

(1) Realize that when a disagreement occurs, it is most important to establish verbal communication.

(2) Be aware that you are moving away from people, isolating yourself from others. The healthy thing is to move toward other people.

(3) Break the cycle; you cannot afford the luxury of a bath of self-pity. Trample those self-indulgent feelings under foot.

(4) Quit blaming everyone else for this situation; accept your portion of the blame.

Silence works two ways. Creatively used it motivates conversation, provides experiences of self-discovery, reveals compassion and concern, and provides the most widely used of all therapeutic tools. Misused silence spells out a certain message of antagonism, defiance, and hatred.

Jack Benny, one of the funniest entertainers in vaudeville, radio, stage, and television, built his career more on silence than on speech. His wit was punctuated with pauses—not silences of scorn—which were more elegant than his gags. His humor was never caustic and attacking but gentle and teasing.

Any would-be helper of other members of the family could well emulate Benny and build a career around creative silence.

OVER ⟶ TO ⟶ YOU

Here is an example of a communication contract between husband and wife.

COMMUNICATION CONTRACT

We the undersigned, being parties to this agreement, each hereby agree:

I AGREE communication is the basis of a good marriage relationship, and I will embark on a course of action to build up our interpersonal communications.

I AGREE to be as honest with both you and myself as I possibly can be. I will withhold no information about my behavior, either before or since we married. You have full right to know the person you married.

I AGREE that I will listen to your remarks and comments without interrupting you. When it is my turn to talk, I expect the same courtesy.

I AGREE that I will first look for things to criticize about myself before I criticize you. Before I complain to you, I will name some fault of mine that, if corrected, would make me a better marriage partner.

I AGREE that sex is a significant level of communication and that I have a sexual obligation in our marriage. Our sexual relations will never be used as a means of reward or punishment.

I AGREE that direct communication is desirable, and I will try not to use ambivalent language or talk through the children, but specifically say what I mean.

I AGREE that communication proceeds best on a verbal level, and I will not try to send messages by banging doors or other nonverbal means.

I AGREE not to use silence as a means of punishing or defying you but as a means of encouraging you to express yourself.

I AGREE not to expect miracles in the improvement of our marriage. There is a great deal you need to know about me and I about you before we can consider ourselves truly married. But I will make every effort toward mutual knowledge and understanding.

I AGREE on the assumption that example is the most persuasive form of argument known to man, that I will diligently seek to improve myself and my communication skills so I can grow into a continually better model of a marriage mate.

Husband————————

Date————————   Wife————————

8. Low Booster Power

*Type D4 Distortions: Family Members Fail
to Make Responses That
Would Motivate the
Speaker*

For many years people living in low-lying areas or areas distant from television stations have been denied television reception because of the technical difficulties involved in getting a signal to them. Now has come a new day with the advent of CATV (Community Antenna Television). This new technique involves positioning powerful antennas on high points of land or on tall structures. These antennas draw in the signals of weak or distant stations, clarify and amplify them, then transmit the signals to the homes of the subscribers to the system.

Boosters, such as are used in CATV, are important parts of any communications system that travels any distance. In family communication Type D Distortions occur when there are no boosters to strengthen the signals as they pass from transmitter to receiver.

To increase the booster power in family communications we need to:

1. Remain on task.
2. Use the family as a training unit.
3. Have fun and games with communication.
4. Learn to ask a question carefully.
5. Develop some good responses.

Remain on Task

Try a quiz.

The most effective way to prevent a person from delivering messages is to:

[ ] a. Heckle him?
[ ] b. Make angry replies?
[ ] c. Refuse to look at him?

The correct answer is "c"—Refuse to look at him. Believe it or not, ignoring a person is the most effective way to stifle his efforts at communication.

My first experience at addressing a black church congregation was a revelation. It happened on a Sunday afternoon, and I was introduced by an elderly gentleman who said, "They say there isn't enough fire in the pulpit these days. The real problem is that there is not enough kindling in the pew." He paused, "Give him some kindling," and the congregation responded with kindling in the form of an enthusiastic fusillade of "amens."

I can't remember when I ever delivered a more forceful and enthusiastic speech, peppered with a flurry of responses from my audience.

That evening I spoke in one of the city's most sophisticated churches where everything was done so precisely and formally with dignity and decorum. My speech was equally precise and formal and, I fear, uninspiring. As I spoke, I mentally speculated as to whether my audience were really alive or just propped-up cadavers.

The attention of my listeners made the difference. By their responses my black friends indicated they were following along with me and boosted my utterance. My silent white congregation effectively cooled me off.

Learning to pay attention is never easy. On one occasion I had been conducting a conference at which I had given five lectures. My wife accompanied me. When we returned to our motel room at night, she suggested we have a dish of ice cream, and I petulantly responded, "Honey, I don't feel like going. I'm tired; I had to lecture five times today."

My little wife looked at me and immediately responded, "What's wrong with you? I had to listen five times today."

She was right. It had probably taken much more work for her to remain "on task" than for me to give my oft-repeated lecture.

It takes a lot of work for the members of a family to learn to really pay attention to someone who is trying to communicate within the particular family unit.

Utilizing Your Family As a Training Unit

As we will notice later, formal educational procedures have virtually ignored oral communication skills. The family as a time-honored educational unit may have to step in and take up the slack by teaching our children techniques to develop these skills.

The very best way to teach children to be effective communicators is to show them how to do it. Aural imitation may be the key to our problem. A child learns by imitation, and he needs a good model by which to fashion himself. Studies have shown that college students who excel in listening come from homes where the parents were thoughtful listeners.

You must demonstrate the communication process. Unite the two processes in one activity. Listen to the children to help them discover their own potential, and as you listen, provide the model for them to follow in learning to listen.

I know a woman who is remarkably effective in relating to people. Shortly after introduction to them she says, "Tell me about yourself."

Some people are so shocked they can't answer immediately, but when they get going, they do remarkably well and generally think highly of her.

This may give us a clue about approaching children. Some

people maintain that the magic words of relationship with children are, "Tell me."

By this simple statement we are saying, "I want to know about you; you are important to me; I am interested in you."

If you notice a child when he is obviously anxious about something, you can make an offer of a listening ear. "You are worried about something?" "Something has upset you." "Would you care to share it with me?"

Remember too the effectiveness of the short reply. Hold up every impulse to jump in and lecture. Try using *yes, uh-huh, uh,* and *I see.*

Watch for nonverbal communication. Look for the child's hands, his voice, facial expressions, stance and bodily movements; all may indicate something of the struggle which is going on within.

After one of these sessions try some evaluation with your child:

(1) What have we been trying to do in these periods?

(2) Did you like people to listen to you?

(3) Do you realize mother and father want to hear what you have to say?

(4) Can you see the way you can help other people by listening to them?

Fun and Games with Communication

Someone has said that one of the problems of modern family life is that the members have lost the ability to entertain themselves. The family of yesterday without TV, radio, or much of the canned amusement of our day frequently spent time playing parlor games. Today parlor games seem to have virtually disappeared.

If you follow the proposals here suggested, you will have some family experiences of playing games, and at the same time the family members will learn some new communication skills.

The Echo Game can be played in almost any situation—

sitting at the table eating, at the conclusion of the meal, traveling in the car, or at a special family gathering. Like all these types of games, it is probably best played when the members can sit in a place where they can see one another.

Commence by selecting a subject. With teenagers, you can use current events, spectator sports, dating, and similar topics. If the ages are younger, try pets, hobbies, or outings. Start the game by announcing the topic. You might then proceed to make some provocative or way-out statement designed to evoke response. Call for some opinions about it. Let it proceed for a short time, and when you feel that it is getting underway, initiate them into the process.

You could say, "We have just been through the first stage of the Echo Game, now we are moving into the second stage. From this time on, whenever you want to speak, please begin by repeating what the previous speaker has just said. If he agrees that you caught on to his idea, you are free to continue the discussion and to make a statement of your own."

After you have been around the group, open the gathering up for discussion. How did you feel? Was it hard really to understand what someone else was saying? What have you learned about listening to another person?

Ask a Question, But do It Carefully

Some questions can ruin a conversation. Take the case of Billy Hespers telling his guests about a remarkable man who used to live down the street. As he relates the story of this man's hunting prowess, Billy takes a few liberties with the facts and exaggerates the number of birds his friend shot on a particular day.

Mrs. Hespers, sitting in the group, has a puzzled look on her face, "Who was this hunter, dear?"

Billy looks embarrassed and mutters, "Tracy Hancock," and never quite gets back on the track again.

Children are given to this activity, and when mother or father relates an incident with anonymous characters, a child can with devastating insistence demand, "Who *was* that, mother?"

Never mind about questions that are checking up on the facts. They may spoil everything. Let the speaker save his face. Use your questions to provoke rather than to slow down conversation.

The technique has potentialities as indicated by the poet in his verse:

> Question Mark
> Behold the Wicked Little Barb
> Which catches fish in human garb.

A group of men sat in a barber's shop, gazing into space, each thinking his own thoughts and inwardly hoping his turn for tonsorial attention might soon arrive.

A bright-eyed youth smiled as he entered, took his seat, and surveyed the zombies lining the wall. After a few futile efforts to get a conversation started, he addressed a question to the farthest barber, "How would you like to work on just heads without bodies?"

The barber pondered a moment and chuckled. Some of the waiting customers looked up. At the end of the shop, a man, obviously anxious to get back to his work, interjected a thought, "Maybe they'll come up with an idea that will let people leave their heads at the shop while they continue their jobs at the office."

The sandy-haired youth in the center joined in, "Wouldn't it be good if you could get a spare head?"

A man whose small edging of fluff around the periphery of baldness only barely justified his presence in the shop wistfully commented, "It might even be possible to trade in your head on a new one."

In short order a stimulating conversaton was under way. Strangers were talking to each other, smiling and laughing.

On one side sat the youth who had started it all. He said nothing, just smiled with a quiet satisfaction. He was now the listener who had started a fascinating conversation with one "way-out" inquiry.

An imaginative question had universal appeal. The harrassed barbers, trying to keep up their work, and the long-suffering customers, thinking of all they needed to do, were all ready to respond to an unusual question.

The late President Kennedy was widely known for his witty answers to questions fired at him. It is not such common knowledge that he also had a peculiar ability to ask an incisive question and pay unusual attention to what was said to him. Robert Saudek conferred with the president while producing the television series, "Profiles in Courage," and later reported: "He made you think he had nothing else to do except ask you questions and listen—with extraordinary concentration—to your answers. You knew that for the time being he had blotted out both the past and the future. More than anyone else I have ever met, President Kennedy seemed to understand the importance of *now*."[1]

"The importance of *now*" is a phrase which conveys the skill of the questioner. His subject becomes vividly aware of this moment when he has something special to contribute in response to the question.

Develop Some Good Responses

Franklin D. Roosevelt led his country through World War II by using a unique communication style. He showed himself to be a conversationalist of the highest order and used *conversation power* to lead his nation.

He contrasted vividly with Winston Churchill, the other famous World War II leader. Both of them used radio, but while Churchill delivered his grandiloquent orations, Roosevelt utilized an entirely different intimate syle in the radio messages he referred to as "Fireside Chats."

In these conversations Roosevelt put himself into the role of a father talking to his children. The nation was one large family, and daddy sitting by the fire opened his heart to his people and shared the national problems with them. He consciously tried to visualize that family of his, and one who observed him in action noted, "His head would nod and his hands move in simple natural comfortable gestures. His face would smile and light up as though he were actually sitting on the front porch or in the parlor with them." The leader who guided the United States through many of the most critical moments in the nation's history maintained his democratic leadership and communicated with his people in his conversational style.

In his face-to-face meetings with people President Roosevelt was a real charmer. He had the capacity to make people feel important, and he did this by the way he listened and responded to what they said.

Frank Capra, the celebrated movie producer, spent some time with the president and describes the way in which he entered into a conversation.

". . . with a big friendly smile, and the glint of intense interest in his sparkling eyes, he would encourage you to talk about yourself, your family, your work, anything. 'Well, I declare!' he'd exclaim after you'd made some inane statement. By little laughs, and goads, and urgings such as 'Really? Tell me more!' . . . 'Well, what do you know!' . . . 'Same thing's happened to me dozens of times!' . . . 'Oh, that's fascinating' . . . his warmth would change you from a stuttering milquetoast to an articulate raconteur."[2]

Small wonder President Roosevelt, the man of the people, was able to marshall the forces of democracy against the tyranny of the axis powers.

Listen for interesting responses. Make a list and memorize them; then when the moment comes, try them out. Notice the way in which they stimulate and enrich communication.

We're living in a day of a variety of boosters. Medicine builds up our powers of resistance to disease; organizations boost the morale of bands and athletic groups; power rockets launch a missile into space; amplifiers beef up a radio or television signal. Let's add another—family communication boosters—and work on this most worthwhile of all booster enterprises.

┌─────────── OVER ⟶ TO ⟶ YOU ───────────┐

A QUIZ FOR QUESTIONERS

Try out your powers of questioning. Some of the following questions are good for boosting communication, and some are poor. Check (√) the good ones, (X) the poor ones.

1. Did you have a good day today?
2. How do you feel about this?
3. Do you like your work?
4. Have you any ideas on the subject?
5. Oh, really?
6. Would you explain this to me?
7. Will you accept the new offer?
8. What is your reaction to this situation?
9. Do you love me?
10. Please give me your opinion on the subject.

After you have concluded, turn to the bottom of the page for the best answers.

GUIDELINES FOR EFFECTIVE QUESTIONING

* Take every possible chance to ask a searching question, *then keep quiet.* (When you're talking, you're not learning anything.)
* One thoughtful question is worth a dozen inquisitive ones. The prod-and-pry approach makes people clam up.
* Questions that come close to the other person's true interest get the best answers—provided you are interested too.
* Be prepared to wait. Sometimes a long silence can be more rewarding than another question.
* In *every case*, the quality of an answer depends on the quality of attention given by the questioner.
* Questions must spring from honest inquiry, not from attempts at flattery or efforts to manipulate the other person's thinking.
* Questions that deal with a person's *feelings* are more provocative than those that deal with *facts*.

ANSWERS TO THE TEST

Questions 1, 3, 5, 7, 9 are poor because they can be answered with a noncommittal yes or no.

Questions 2, 4, 6, 8, 10 are better. They stimulate further conversation.

Roger—Message Received, or Was It?

The message has at last reached the receiver—a family member's receptor organs—but it still has five hefty hurdles to leap.

9. Getting the Message

*Type E Distortions: Family Members Don't
Hear What's Said*

The most prestigious of all athletic events is a foot race exactly twenty-six miles, three hundred eighty-five yards in length. The fabled Marathon gets its distance from a notable event in Grecian history. When the Greeks won a victory over the Persians in 490 B.C., the young Greek, Pheidippides, ran from Marathon to Athens, a distance of twenty-eight miles, three hundred eighty-five yards, to carry the news of Grecian success.

As the storied athlete raced into the city of Athens he shouted the joyous tidings, "Rejoice, we conquer," then stumbled, fell, and died of exhaustion. Like Pheidippides, the message transmitted by a member of the family may have fought off all the Type D Distortions that challenge as it passes along the channel only to collapse at the ears, eyes, or other receptor organs of the other family member.

Type E Distortions take a number of different forms, and the condition of the receptor organs can complicate the receiving process.

Children are notorious for their inability to hear what their parents are saying, and there may be some plain, ordinary physical reasons for this. They may have lost at least some of their ability to hear. Otologists, who specialize in hearing problems, are reporting that the years of electronically amplified rock-and-roll music are taking their toll on the rising generation's hearing.

Researchers point out that the level of sound in some rock-

and-roll night clubs may reach as high as one hundred twenty-five decibels. One interested medical man picked up his teen-age daughter from a dance. In the course of the car journey home he noticed she wasn't hearing what he was saying. Curiosity aroused, the doctor paid a visit to a dance and set up some monitoring equipment. Tests revealed that the sound in front of the band peaked at one hundred twenty decibels. Further tests following the conclusion of the dance indicated that despite their youthful resilience, the kids showed an average hearing loss of eleven decibels, and one boy showed a thirty-five decibel loss.

When junior, in response to the question, "Why didn't you do what I told you?" responds, "I didn't hear you," there's a chance he may be reporting the results of years of exposure to ear-splitting rock-and-roll music.

This phenomenon is not confined to children. Mary Telfer has a growing sense of frustration about her spouse's lack of responsiveness to many of her choicest statements. Within herself she sometimes nurtures the growing conviction he "just ignores me." It could possibly have something to do with his military service.

A man who joins the U.S. Army lays his life on the line and despite excellent medical services may suffer injuries that will incapacitate him for the rest of his days. The gravest danger he faces is that his ears may be hurt. U.S. Army authorities report that hearing is the number one occupational hazard for all combat troops; in fact, noise-induced hearing loss may be the army's single greatest health hazard. It has been conservatively estimated that from 30 to 50 percent of all active duty army personnel suffer some noise-induced hearing loss during their military careers. For some, the effects are temporary; for others, the loss is permanent.

Not only does the soldier face the problem when on active duty, his leisure hours may still confront him with the hazard. Investigations into entertainment provided for the troops have shown the damage caused by loud music in recreation centers. One serious suggestion has been to attach electronic sensors or squelch devices on sound equipment used in many service clubs. These devices will turn on warning lights or shut down the sound emitter if the noise exceeds the limits of safety.

The Veteran's Administration reports that it pays more than fifty million dollars annually in compensation for service-connected hearing losses.

When you see a U.S. soldier wearing a small plastic container with two plugs enclosed and attached to his jacket, remember it is no whim or doodad for prettying up his uniform. It indicates the army's concern for his hearing.

Despite all these precautions, one artillery officer's wife describes a social conversation of a group of artillery officers as resembling a shouting match. It readily follows that there's a potentiality for Type E Distortions in a marriage relationship between people whose ears may have suffered in this way.

Other receptor organs are vulnerable. John Hartman, a student in Temple University's School of Medicine, has developed a new way of studying anatomy—by touch. He doesn't even look at the body upon which he is working, but plunges his hands into the cadaver and by handling bones and organs learns their shape, location, and distinctive feeling. The reason is that John is blind. He is the first sightless student to be accepted by a medical school in this century. At last report he was in the top quarter of his class.

Barbara Walters, nationally known television personality, told of an unusual interview with poet Robert Smithdas. The conversation proceeded as the deaf and blind Smithdas placed his thumb on Miss Walter's lips.

John Hartman learning and Smithdas getting a message by touch remind us that humans receive communications by a number of routes: hearing, seeing, smelling, touching, and tasting, among others. By their very nature these receptors are open to interference.

When Mrs. McDonald returns home unexpectedly and notices a peculiar odor in the house, she asks her seventeen-year-old Jimmy what has been happening. Jimmy replies he has had a couple of friends over to listen to records, and Harry Thompson brought some incense to burn as they listened. Jimmy's message is distorted by his mother's sensory perceptions which bring her the message that her son may have been using marijuana.

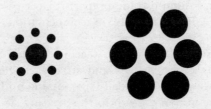

Are the center circles the same?

Other senses are equally vulnerable. Look at the two dots in the illustration, and as you examine them you will realize that the setting of the dots has a lot to do with the visual message we receive. Jan Sterling becomes aware of this. As her husband returns from the business convention in San Francisco, he tells her, "I hardly had a single moment to myself." But later as she unpacks his clothes and sees some red markings on his shirt collar, she does some interpreting. It could be they were just some impressions from the red crayons used on his charts, but considering what she's heard about conventions and the goings on there, there's always the possibility that they might be . . . lipstick?

In husband-wife relations the anticipatory set may mean the subject is in a state of readiness to respond in an accustomed manner. As the signal reaches the receiver, the response comes almost as a reflex action. The problem lies in the receiver not being nearly as knowledgeable as he imagined.

One television show has popularized a game in which husbands and wives are separated from each other. Then the wife is asked to say what she believes her husband's ideas are on a given subject or how he will respond to a certain situation. In an unusual number of cases the answer is *wrong*.

These experiences are an example of the *basic false assumption of marriage*: Most husbands and wives labor under the delusion that they have a clear insight into their spouse's mental processes and reactions. This just *isn't* true.

Whenever I hear a woman say, "My husband believes . . . ," my internal reaction is, "I wonder what he would think if he could hear this statement."

Working with troubled marriages I frequently make a suggestion about a course of action and then say, "I would like your husband to come along."

The wife responds, "He'll not come. You don't know my husband."

I reply, "I've never met your husband, but I know him better than you. If you'll follow the plan I propose, there are nine chances out of ten that he will come."

And it generally works out that way. This lack of knowledge of a spouse is one of the most aggravating aspects of trying to help troubled marriages.

Steve Kinkaid, talking with his wife, braces himself, then says, "Okay, go ahead, get it off your chest, but I know exactly what you're going to say."

He puts on the appearance of a householder battening down for a hurricane and sits with a look that defies his spouse to produce a convincing argument.

The "anticipatory set" means many a message from a spouse is cut off at the receiver level. Emotional factors may be responsible for Type E Distortions.

Mrs. Jean Fabian was being interviewed by her psychotherapist. As she spoke of her difficulty in making a satisfactory sexual adjustment in marriage, she recounted an experience of childhood days. She and her sister shared a bed, and one night during the absence of her mother from the home, her father had joined the girls in bed and began to make sexual overtures to Jean. Completely scared by her father's alcoholic breath and his amorous approaches, she jumped out of bed and rushed out the door and down the street to the home of a friend. She made the excuse that mother was away and she had become frightened and asked if she could spend the night with them.

All that long night she kept worrying about her sister and what was happening back in the bedroom. The next day after her mother's return she went back to the house but did not discuss the events of the previous evening with her sister.

The years passed, and Jean often wondered about that night. Both sisters were now married, and on one occasion they were together visiting. Jean raised the question as to what had happened that night. Her sister responded and Mrs. Fabian reported, "I sat and looked at her. Her lips were moving, but I couldn't hear a sound she said."

Mrs. Fabian's emotional trauma and guilt over her action on that night had interfered with her receiving the message from her sister.

A similar illustration as to the way guilt may affect perception is seen in the biblical incident of Amnon and Tamar. Amnon, attracted to his beautiful half-sister, finally trapped her in his house and seduced her. Following the seduction he cast her out of the house. The Bible tells us that before the event Amnon "loved her"; following the sexual episode, "Amnon hated her exceedingly; so that the hatred wherewith he hated her was greater than the love wherewith he had loved her" (2 Sam. 13: 15 King James Version). The guilt of his act caused a complete change in Amnon's perception of Tamar.

Type E Distortions must be controlled because they all too easily garble an incoming message and deprive us of many of the increments family life should bring.

Traveling to a speaking engagement in the mountains of West Virginia, I had arrived by plane at the airport to be met by my host. As we drove down the mountain road, my host's keen eyes espied skid marks on the pavement. He pulled over and scrambled down the slope, calling to me to stay where I was while he investigated.

It turned out a car had run off the road and was overturned at the base of the twenty-foot incline. My friend managed to get the car door open and assisted two women and a baby from the vehicle. None of them was seriously injured.

As I joined in the rescue effort, I helped the mother and her baby to climb the slope to the road. The woman sobbed hysterically. As I tried to alleviate her distress, I pointed out that she and the baby were both safe.

I will never forget the moment when that frightened little

woman turned her scratched face toward me and in her peculiar mountain accent plaintively voiced her major concern, "But what will my husband say about the car?"

In reality what did the car matter? A grateful husband would probably be pathetically thankful that his wife and family were safe. But their continued interaction had created an anticipatory set in his wife, particularly as far as the automobile was concerned, and left her without the support of her husband in the crisis moment of family life.

OVER ⟶ TO ⟶ YOU

When a family member doesn't seem to be paying attention or can't remember being told, it may not be just inattention. Try some checking.

(1) Your daughter Charlotte is not attentive, doesn't always come when you call. You begin to wonder if she might have a hearing loss. Here are some things you can do.

- (a) Check with the speech and hearing center, and make an appointment to see an audiologist who is qualified to administer a complete audiological examination.
- (b) Consult a medical doctor who specializes in these sorts of difficulties, an otologist or an ear-nose-and-throat-specialist.
- (c) Don't rush to a hearing-aid dealer. Most are reputable but may have an overriding interest in selling the product.

(2) If your spouse is a veteran and seems to be experiencing hearing difficulties, you might try a visit to the VA hospital. Remember, a large proportion of veterans have hearing losses, and he may be eligible for some help with his problem.

(3) Handling guilt may help clarify communication. A good series of steps is:

- (a) Be willing to sit down and ruthlessly examine the situation.
- (b) Accept responsibility. Put aside your ego defenses and accept whatever blame belongs to you.
- (c) Become open—acknowledge failure—to yourself, another person, significant others.
- (d) Undertake some act of restitution. Put things right if you have hurt someone.

10. Strange Things People Hear

Type F1 Distortions: Problems in Understanding What a Family Member Is Trying to Tell You

John and Susan Webster are "anniversary nuts." They celebrate their first date, the night of his proposal, the engagement announcement, and a host of other events having to do with the birth and development of their relationship. Each of these occasions has become a ritualistic gift-swapping experience.

Susan is nudging her husband at the morning hour of awakening, "Honey, it's getting-up time." John stirs and turns a bleary eye on her. She inquires "You remember what day it is, don't you?"

"No, I don't know. What is it?"

"I'm not going to tell you. If you can't remember, well, that's it." Susan's voice has a note of disappointment.

Several times before he left for work, John petitioned his wife to tell him what he should be remembering about today, but she steadfastly refused to enlighten him.

That night as he greeted the light of his life with a kiss, Walter produced a gift-wrapped parcel: "I've tried all day to remember what anniversary it is, and I could not for the life of me recollect, but I've bought a present. Now please tell me what day it is?"

His wife smiled, "It's Thursday, the day you should put the garbage out."

John had heard a different message than the one his wife had meant to pass on.

During World War II, the German intelligence agency known as ABWER developed a unique method for sending and receiving messages from their special agents. In addition to the normal paper and pencil codes, German chemists perfected *G-Tinten* or special inks. The formula for these was amongst the most closely guarded secrets of the German intelligence.

A spy, code-named Hamlet, functioning in Mozambique in Portugues East Africa, kept track of allied shipping by utilizing the chemicals to disguise the messages he sent to his headquarters.

While Hamlet was writing messages, obliterating them with the chemicals, then transmitting the expunged documents, he did well. But due to a slip-up in the organization, someone had failed to supply him with the formula of the reagents that would make the writing reappear on the documents.

After unsuccessful efforts to send a courier with the chemicals, ABWER headquarters decided to transmit the formula in a coded cable. This cable gave detailed directions as to how to prepare the chemicals. British censors intercepted the cable and cracked the code giving them the means of chemically treating, reading, and decoding the messages written in the special ink.

Like the spy Hamlet, many members of a family may be very capable in transmitting messages, but when it comes to receiving, they experience great difficulty in decoding the messages from other family members. The success of a communication experience depends upon both processes of encoding and decoding, and the way in which the listener decodes the message is of the utmost importance.

Many factors hinder the process of decoding. One of these is the transmitter's accent, those peculiar patterns of speech so beautifully dramatized in the musical, *My Fair Lady*, in which Henry Higgins is capable of hearing a person speak and immediately stating the country or geographical location from which the speaker comes.

A teacher in Brooklyn was taking her children for an outing in the park. As they walked along, one of the children cried out, "Look up in the tree; it's a boid."

The teacher quickly corrected her student, "'That's not a boid, but it's a bird."

To which the child replied, "That's funny. It sure looked like a boid."

Personally I speak with an accent which betrays my Australian origin and generally gets the attention of the group I address. It brings me such back-handed compliments as, "Even if you didn't say anything worthwhile, your accent would be interesting to listen to." It also gets me a quota of difficulty such as when I was dictating some material on listening and discovered my secretary had typed "renewal account." As this seemed more like an accounting than a psychological term, I checked out my original material which I discovered had been dictated as "neural current."

My secretary's ears, even though long bombarded with my accent, still had difficulty in sorting out some of the sounds.

Words themselves may have a variety of meanings as is seen in the word *run*:

A boy *runs* down the street.
A candidate *runs* when seeking office.
When a stocking is damaged, it *runs*.
An advertisement may be *run* in the paper.
Bank interest grows as it *runs* from January to December.
Time *runs* out at a ball game.
Colors move but little as they *run*.
There can be a *run* on the stock market.
A dress may *run* you $30.
You can enclose your poultry in a chicken *run*.
An easement *runs* through the land.
You may *run* into a friend.

In each of these instances the same word is used, but it has a different meaning depending on the context.

All our decoding in communication must be done in consideration of the many meanings of words. An early Christian father, St. Augustine, said that words do not have intrinsic meaning, "Rather they 'have' a meaning because men have agreed upon it." Words are like the chameleon lizard which changes its color to fit its environment, and words must be interpreted by the context within which they are used. Consequently, in decoding we need to ask what the word means to the encoder and interpret accordingly.

The Peculiar Art of Bypassing

One of the strangest quirks of communication is the use of humor. Much humor depends on the capacity of the teller of a funny story to lay the groundwork by deliberately miscommunicating. He leads the listener to believe he's going in one direction, then suddenly turns his story to a completely unexpected ending. The surprise is so sudden it strikes us as funny and we laugh.

The story of the young couple strolling along on a warm summer evening illustrates the point. As they walked, two sounds came to their ears, the chirping of the crickets and the choir practicing their special music at the church.

Captivated by the lovely music, the young lady remarked, "Isn't that beautiful."

Her male friend, attention focused on the crickets, responded, "Yes, I believe they make that sound by rubbing their hind legs together."

The problem lay in their *apparent agreement* which caused them to *bypass* each other, and bypassing can cause problems in communication.

I discovered this on one occasion in chapel. I took my place among the faculty on the platform from which we could look out over the sea of students. Sitting in the chair by my side was Dr. Carlson. This Scandinavian gentleman really enjoyed talking and was in particularly good form on this occasion, speaking out of the corner of his mouth with comments on the weather, politics, and sundry people present at chapel.

As we sang the first hymn, I noticed an elderly gentleman, casually clad, stick in hand, come wandering into the balcony of the building. In one of those fleeting moments when Dr.

Carlson was not speaking, I asked him, "Who is that old boy who just came into the gallery?"

My seat mate immediately responded, "I. R. Rankin, one of the most famous of all the hymn writers."

That surely set me back. I'd seen that elderly gentleman before and had casually passed him by. It just shows how off-handedly we treat the great of the past.

I scarcely heard the speaker that morning. My mind pondered the gentleman so talented yet treated in such a casual manner. I determined to seek an opportunity in my eleven o'clock class to lecture my students on the subject.

Yet it bothered me. That old gent gave no appearance of scholarship . . . he looked so ordinary.

The chapel service concluded. Dr. Carlson had taken up the subject he'd left earlier. Seeking certainty, I said, "Excuse me for interrupting, Dr. Carlson. I want to verify what you said earlier. Just what hymns were written by that man in the gallery?"

"What man in the balcony?" Dr. Carlson had a startled look on his face.

"Didn't you tell me that old gentleman in the balcony was I. R. Rankin, one of the most famous hymn writers?"

Dr. Carlson looked at me, "What I heard you say was 'Who wrote this hymn?' and I responded it was I. R. Rankin, one of the most famous hymn writers."

Dr. Carlson and I had bypassed each other.

In the domestic situation, bypassing and apparent agreements sometimes give rise to interesting experiences as is seen in the case of Mr. and Mrs. Webster, mentioned at the opening of the chapter. Unfortunately, they can also create monumental marital communication problems.

Don't Help Too Much

Communication depends on the behavior of two people, the one who speaks and the one who listens. The speaker is hard at work encoding, and the listener or listeners are decoding. If the message is to be successfully passed on, there must be agreement between the speaker's encoding and the listener's decoding.

An effective communicator needs some assistance in encoding his message so he will be understood. One of the suggestions sometimes given to a writer or speaker is, "Have some outsider evaluate your ideas." But, of course, if the communicator is married, this problem has been looked after. He has someone—not an outsider (unfortunately?)—who will give him assistance in his encoding activities.

As in a time of national emergency, censors work at checking over information in the media, so many husbands and wives feel they have a similar responsibility for keeping surveillance over their spouse's utterances to make sure that all ideas have been successfully encoded.

Some women, wrapped up in their own little world and happy to leave traveling arrangements and trip planning to their husbands, are not particularly adept at estimating distances. Such a one is Ellen Manz who, when the Manzes are entertaining company, loves to relate some unusual experience that befell the family on their last vacation trip.

Ellen's face lights up as she says, "Last year we decided to really see the United States, and we set out on a forty-thousand-mile trip."

Ed Manz, sitting across the room, flinches at this statement. His reaction is quick and sure. "Wait, honey, four thousand miles." Then he explains to the assembled company, "That's my little wife. She's not sure whether its four miles, four thousand miles, or forty thousand miles."

Although most of us are willing to be courteous and listen to a guest with a forgiving spirit, we have a strange change of attitude with a spouse.

A visitor tells us about a trip to Paducah, Texas, and states the population is 2,150. We know for a fact, having read in the latest edition of the *Texas Almanac*, that Paducah now has 4,000 inhabitants. Do we jump in and put him right? No, most of us are willing to let him miss it by a few thousand and keep the story moving along.

But not so with a spouse. Let there be a discrepancy—no

matter how small—and we feel an obligation to keep the record straight, even though we slow down the story, annoy our guests, and completely frustrate our spouse. Along with this is a peculiar sensitivity to the effect of a spouse's remarks upon other people. Jim Marshall is about to tell the story of the Cajun fisherman who was confused by a bus schedule. He starts, "Have you ever heard the story about the Cajun . . ." He hesitates in response to the head tilting, eyebrow raising of his wife. Something's wrong. So he changes the subject, "Speaking of Cajuns, do you think the New Orleans Saints will have a chance against the Cowboys on Saturday?"

Following the departure of the guests, Jim quizzes his wife, "Why did you give me those quitting signals when I started on the Cajun story?"

"Well, honey, you probably didn't know, but Mr. and Mrs. Knowles both come from Louisiana, and your story might have been offensive to them."

For some peculiar reason, a spouse's remarks are critically examined, and the result is a peculiar, almost paranoid attitude, toward them. It may have something to do with the *pre-post marital paradox*. "Before marriage lovers overlook the faults and magnify each other's virtues. Following marriage the tendency is to magnify the faults and overlook the spouse's virtues."

If family communications are to be developed, we must exercise restraint. Remember the words of Jesus:

"Don't criticize people, and you will not be criticized. For you will be judged by the way you criticize others, and the measure you give will be the measure you receive.

"Why do you look at the speck of sawdust in your brother's eye and fail to notice the plank in your own? How can you say to your brother, 'Let me get the speck out of your eye,' when there is a plank in your own? You fraud! Take the plank out of your own eye first, and then you can see clearly enough to remove your brother's speck of dust" (Matt. 7:1–5, Phillips).

Then there is the simple matter of the courtesies of life. All too frequently we're more considerate with outsiders than we are with fellow family members. Let us treat our family group with at least the same courtesy and consideration we would extend to an outsider whom we are trying to impress.

— OVER ⟶ TO ⟶ YOU —

AVOIDING THE BYPASSING TRAP

* *Be person-minded, not word-minded*—Remember words have different meanings for different people. Never assume a word means the same thing to both you and your listener. Particularly with the children, take time to explain what you mean when you use a word.

* *Query*—If you have any doubt about what is being said, ask the speaker, but do it in a way that will make him look superior to you. "I'm probably a bit dumb on this subject, and I don't seem to be getting what you're saying. Could you please explain what you mean?"

* *Try paraphrasing*—In some business conferences once a participant has made a statement the moderator repeats the idea as he understands it. Remember the echo game with your children. Don't be afraid to say, "As I understand it, you are saying . . ." Then give the speaker a chance to respond.

* *Be willing to explain*—Don't cut off a family member who needs some additional information. It might well be they ought to know or should have listened, but they don't and didn't. Remember your communication has entirely failed if they have not received it clearly. Take a bit of time.

* *Fight back the impulse to correct your spouse*—You are probably the only one who noticed the misinformation, exaggeration, or impulsive statement. Remember the common courtesy you would extend to anyone else. Be at least willing to do as much for your partner.

* *If you want to do some bypassing, try it with your funny stories*—That way you can have your satisfaction and entertain as well.

11. The Emotional Short Circuit

Type F2 Distortions: A Family Member Blows a Fuse and Misses the Message

Mrs. Polly Pearson prides herself on her efficiency, but this particular day makes her wonder just how much a woman can take. The day began badly with the household oversleeping which led to a frantic breakfast rush, followed by Polly's car-pool responsibility. Shortly after she returned home, the school nurse called to suggest Polly take Nancy to the doctor. A frustrating wait in the doctor's office led to an okay of her daughter's health, "Just a virus. Give her a couple of aspirin and keep her warm." This incident was followed by a mad dash to the women's club to engage in a strenuous debate over the new ~onstitution. With a rising anxiety level Polly rushes to pick up the kids from school, stops to pay the utility bill, and then dashes madly into the house to be greeted with the smell of the stew being burned up on the stove.

When her husband, Roger, completely unaware of everything that has happened, enters the house to query her, "What, no dinner ready? What have you been doing with yourself all day?" Polly turns on him and pours out a flood of invective. He responds in kind.

Polly and Roger are learning that emotional short circuits play an important role in family communication.

In his book, *Witness*, Whittaker Chambers tells of an experience which led him to abandon his atheism and ultimately his membership in the Communist party. Standing one night and looking down at his sleeping daughter, he was overwhelmed by the beautifully intricate formation of her ear. He finally concluded, "No, these ears were not created by chance."[1]

Any inquirer who pauses to consider the subject of human auscultation—the act of listening—must not only be impressed by the shape of the ear but also the whole complex functioning of human audition.

The mechanism of the ear itself is made up of three parts: the external ear, the middle ear, and the inner ear. All play a peculiar role in the hearing process.

The outer ear includes the delicately sculptured and arranged auricle, a trumpet which catches the sound waves and guides them into a passage of about one and one-half inches called the auditory channel. The outer third of this channel is lined with tiny, wax-producing glands and fine hairs that constitute a gentle but effective barrier to discourage inquisitive insects and keep out foreign bodies.

Separating the outer ear from the middle ear is the eardrum, or tympanic membrane, a thin sheet of tissue about one-quarter of an inch in diameter. Sound waves vibrate the eardrum which in turn touches the first of three movable bones closely linked to each other. Called the auditory ossicles, these bones are of unusual shapes which have given them their picturesque names. Attached to the eardrum is the malleus or hammer, which rests against the incus or anvil that in turn impinges on the stapes or stirrup.

To the hammer, anvil, and stirrup is added a snail-shaped mechanism, the cochlea, known more popularly as the inner ear. Sound vibrations move the stapes or stirrup in and out of an oval window in the cochlea disturbing the liquid called perilymph which vibrates some of the twenty-four thousands fibers of the basilar membrane and stimulates the attached nerves.

From this "Organ of Corti," as it is called, the impulse enters the enormously complex human nervous system which may be compared to a huge telephone system in which there are miles of wires. If a telephone system did not have some central switchboard, it would be unable to function.

Similarly man's nervous system has miles of neural fibers

which connect with the central coordinating structure we call the brain. The surface of the brain is "convoluted," so called because it looks like hills and valleys pushed closely together. It is divided into two halves called hemispheres, each of which has two lobes, and one of these is the temporal lobe to which the message from the ear is transmitted.

The cortex or "bark" of the brain is gray in color and covered with a tremendous number of neurons which are interrelated and provide a fantastic number of circuits that can be hooked up allowing the neural current to be routed in a great variety of directions.

The possibility of distortion enters. The incoming message which should have had calm, rational consideration may short-circuit so that the recipient reacts in a fast, gut-level, nonrational manner.

Emotional Early-Warning System

Harry Fontaine is hanging a picture for his wife. An industrious businessman, he is the despair of his mate when it comes to household chores. In fact, he rather prides himself on his lack of domestic skills and often brags that he doesn't know which end of the hammer to hold. But today it is different.

By leaving the picture in an obvious place where he had nearly fallen over it, his helpmate had been able to offer a subtle suggestion and then appear pleasantly surprised when he walked in carrying his seldom-used tools and announced his intention to "get this picture on the wall."

The little woman works hard at keeping him motivated.

"Honey, that's wonderful. Not only the best businessman in the city but a handyman as well," she murmurs.

"Oh, shucks, it's nothing." But Harry has a pretty good feeling. "How's that? Seems like a pretty good spot to me."

He holds the picture in a trial position and awaits the final word of approval.

"Just a bit too high, honey. Mother always said you had high ideas . . ."

Harry's interest in picture hanging evaporates. He labors

through the rest of the chore in the most half-hearted manner. "Mother always said . . ." does something to Harry.

Like so many of us, Harry has an Emotional Early-Warning System. As soon as some words cross the threshold of our hearing, the red lights flash and the alarm bells begin to clang.

The very moment some Republicans hear "Democrat" or an industrialist hears "union," or there comes to our ears a name or concept about which we feel strongly, the Emotional Early-Warning System goes into action.

Even such a highly developed and intricate radar system as that spreading across North America can misinterpret a harmless object as being a threatening invader. A man's Emotional Early-Warning System may be triggered by one word and prevent him from hearing the rest of the statement.

The wife's word *mother* may fire an explosion and keep hubby from hearing that his mother-in-law has drawn her will in his favor. A message that the representative from the Internal Revenue Department would like an interview can lead to a noncooperative response which will keep the professional man from learning there is a better way to figure his income tax.

One researcher in the industrial field gives an example of the Emotional Early-Warning System in industry. The foreman greets one of his men: "How's the job coming, George?"

Interpretation 1—Simon Legree is checking up on me again."

Interpretation 2—"He's really interested in how I'm doing."

Interpretation 3—"Oh—oh, has he found out that I punched Bill Mott's time card this morning?"

Number 2 might have been the true interpretation, but George will never know, and it doesn't matter what his foreman says, for it will always be misinterpreted.

The good communicator faces the reality of the Emotional Early-Warning System and works at developing techniques for handling this troublesome distortion point in family communication. Here are some pointers:

Distrust your initial reactions. Some people boast about the accuracy of first impressions, but most of these are notoriously inaccurate.

Fight for time before you respond. Don't make impulsive responses.

Forget about the appearance of irritating manner, accent, bombastic or self-effacing attitude. Don't think so much of *who* is speaking but *what* he is saying.

If certain words or ideas upset you, write them down and examine them carefully. Ask yourself why. Discuss them with a friend.

Be willing to evaluate a new or unusual idea. Try to see both sides.

As much as you may dislike the idea that you hear, look for some positive aspects of it.

Control by Tantrum

Few of us can witness a violent expression of emotions and not be awed by it. Children learn this early in life and proceed to take advantage of the technique of intimadating by crying, screaming, holding their breath, kicking, and punching. Many parents feel completely helpless in the face of these emotional outbursts and capitulate to the child's demands, thus rewarding him and reinforcing his behavior. Children learn quickly and rapidly master the skill of *managing by tantrum*. The lesson so learned may be carried over into later life.

The child-learner may now become the child-teacher and turn on his or her parents, teaching them the skills of managing by tantrum. Mrs. Burns, mother of three, aged eight, seven, and five respectively, sometimes gets the impression that her family is in a perpetual state of riot. She keeps urging the children, "Hold it down," but they pay little or no attention to her pleas. When she can stand it no longer, she steadily begins to raise her voice until she finds herself yelling.

Mrs. Burns confides in her friend Mrs. Zimmerman, "After it's all over I feel bad about it, all stirred up, head aching, and I wonder how much the people in the other apartments heard. But it seems to be the only way I can control them."

The children have taught Mrs. Burns to communicate strong emotional expressions as a means of managing her offspring and sometimes seem to take particular pleasure in provoking mother to these expressions.

Most people in the common experiences of relationship at their places of employment or social events keep their emotions under control, but when they get home the restraints are off, and the situation may be quite different.

Mr. Robert Green's work, for example, is demanding, and he tries to be fair in his dealings with the other employees, but his frustrations mount. When he gets home, he has a very low irritation level.

The Green household has learned about daddy's hair-trigger reaction, so Mrs. Green prepares the family for father's return, making sure the paper is in place near his favorite chair and that all the children are warned of his approach. Green is surprised when his brother Harold comes to stay with them a few days and comments on Green's entrance into the house: "I've gotta give it to you, Robert, you've really trained your family. As Patty [Mrs. Green] gets them ready for your entrance, 'Be sure your father's chair is in the right place,' 'Where's the paper?' 'Don't make any noise when daddy arrives,' I have a feeling some oriental potentate is being given a royal welcome."

The remark leaves Robert with a strange feeling about the way in which he arrives home. He begins to question his attitude and the image he is communicating to the members of his family.

For those who require it, a beautiful rationalization is at hand, and it has an apparently sound psychological theory behind it.

Harrison Taylor is annoyed with Genevieve, his wife, who has finally admitted overspending the budget so she could get the cute little dresses on sale at Nieman Marcus.

"But, honey, can't you see I saved fifty dollars by buying while they were on sale?"

"Saved fifty dollars! What nonsense! I am sick to death of spending money to save money."

"Do you want your wife to go around wearing old clothes?"

"My dear, you've got more clothes than any other three

women. There are dresses in your closet that you've never worn twice."

"I'm surprised at you, Harrison, but I should have known. You have always been a tightwad."

"What do you mean a tightwad?"

So the exchange gets more heated at Harrison and Genevieve's house as they enter into a verbal slug fest.

The following evening they have a long talk, and Genevieve snuggles up to Harrison, "I'm so glad I took those psychology courses. Isn't it good the way we can really express ourselves and drain off our emotions? Our quarrel has been a therapeutic experience."

Taylor—still hurting at the memory of Genevieve's facile and tart tongue that was able to deliver stinging blows—wonders.

The validity of Genevieve's idea that expression of emotions helps to drain them has both proponents and opponents.

There are some good reasons to doubt this premise. From observations it seems that constant expression of emotions not only doesn't drain the emotions but may reinforce these reactions. If action brings on feeling, this may simply bring on a more intensive feeling.

Add to this the effect we have on others.

Take the case of Charla and Jack Donovan. Jack has a hair-trigger reaction, and this in turn sparks something in Charla. In telling her story Charla says, "He gets mad and flies off at me. I stand it for a while, then I become vividly aware of the injustice of his attitude, and I strike back at him. The situation deteriorates, and sometimes we stay mad at each other for several days, and it all started over a triviality."

This is the tragedy of people who believe in expressing their emotions. A family is an interacting unit. In the process of expressing emotions the people that get hurt are the ones that we love most of all.

How should we go about handling these angry feelings that block our communication? A seven-fold program might help:

(1) Recognize you are angry or emotionally upset. It is part of the business of living. "Be angry and sin not."

(2) Pinpoint the reason for your anger. Realize who you are mad at. Don't project anger about the office to your wife and children who had nothing to do with these situations. If you are often mad at yourself, face your own foolish mistakes.

(3) Don't be a martyr. You must accept some responsibility for what has happened. William Blake, speaking about anger, said:

> I was angry with my friend,
> I told my wrath, my wrath did end.
> I was angry with my foe
> I told him not, my wrath did grow.

What did this anonymous person tell his friend? If he pointed out his own irresponsibility and said in all honesty, "I have looked over my behavior and I can see I made some wrong moves," he probably would soon feel better.

Accept your own humanness. Realize when you have failed, and you will feel a lot better about the situation.

(4) Try physical activity. An emotional arousal is a preparation for physical activity. This mechanism prepared primitive man to fight or flee; you may be able to do neither. Work off the adrenaline that has readied your body. Try a walk, jog, work-out in the gym. One salesman reported a visit to the driving range where he saw obstreperous clients' faces on the balls as he banged away at them. He worked off an emotion and might just have improved his game in the process.

(5) Keep short accounts with your family. If there is an explosion, patch it up as soon as possible. Don't let it drag on for days with the whole household under an emotional cloud. Every family should adopt the principle, "Let not the sun go down on your wrath."

(6) Try a decisive motivational action. Remember the saying, "It is much easier to act yourself into a new way of feeling than to feel yourself into a new way of acting." Act, then feel. If you don't feel it, deliberately break the cycle; square your shoulders, put a smile on your face, and move toward people.

(7) Clarify your communication. An emotional short circuit is conveying a message, but it is distorted and indistinct and

open to a variety of interpretations. Communicate verbally.
Put your message into words.

Accepting Criticism

What would be the best single technique for developing
a good harmonious family relationship? The judicious use of
criticism. That is, if we are to believe Nordoff.

This investigator carried out research on thirty communities
of the nineteenth century. In these communities the members
lived together in a closeness that even involved sharing all
their worldly goods. Being at such close quarters these people
soon discovered their "heavens on earth" weren't paradises
after all, and they needed some techniques by which they
could learn to live amicably together.

Nordoff concluded from his research that one group, the
Oneida community, also called the Perfectionists, had developed the best method of all for keeping harmony and peace
among the members. "For this purpose I know of no better
means that that which the Perfectionists call 'criticism'—
telling a member to his face, in regular and formal meeting,
what is the opinion of his fellows."

Nordhoff turned family-life educator and went on to suggest an extension of the idea to the domestic sphere: "This
'criticism,' kindly and conscientiously used, would be an excellent means of discipline in most families, and would in almost
all cases abolish scolding and grumbling."

While Nordhoff's ideas may have some validity, Type F
Distortions may enter to nullify the effectiveness of using
criticism.

Human beings have shown a remarkable capacity to take
punishment. They have managed to survive terrible ordeals—
wars, plaques, illnesses, starvation—but none of these is the
supreme test of man's spirit. This trial is reserved for a more
suitable ordeal which shows real capacity to suffer and endure
—the way he can take criticism.

We have all met a self-sufficient individual who, when told

that someone has printed a criticism of him, responds, "Did
they spell my name correctly?"

Even though some of us more sensitive spirits have an ad-
miration for this capacity to "take it" and may envy his calm
aplomb, we have a sneaking suspicion that he is somewhat
egotistical and insensitive.

Most of us feel a stinging blow to our self-love when someone points out our faults, failings, or foibles, especially in the
presence of others. Yet it is of utmost importance that we know
how we appear to other people. The famous Scottish poet
breathed the prayer that contains such a vital truth:

> O wad some Power the giftie gie us
> To see oursels as ithers see us!
> It wad frae monie a blunder free us.

Such is our capacity for self-deception that few humans
would really pray this prayer for themselves. But the poet-
observer of the passing scene recognized how badly most of
us really need a critic.

President Johnson was known as a man not overly fond of
criticism. Who is for that matter? One of his subordinates
made the point that Mr. Johnson did at least listen, though he
had a peculiar style in even this procedure. He told of the
president's way of dealing with one of his staff members who
questioned or criticized some presidential policy or proposal.

"Does he listen? He listens so hard it's deafening—it's like
being at the bottom of a lake, the pressure's so high. He sits
slumped down and stares at you—he hardly ever blinks, you
know. Then if you're just rambling on, and you come to a
lame conclusion, he says, 'Therefore?' and you say 'Therefore,
we ought to do thus-and-so,' but you'd better make it sound
convincing or he just looks at you and sort of shrugs you off."

But he did listen to their criticism.

You're going to get criticism. Don't let Type F Distortions
rob you of this experience. Learn to listen and to take it.

Listening to criticism does two things. If the criticism is
unjust and unfair, you may disarm the critic. If the criticism

is justified, you have really learned something. You stand to gain on both counts if you listen.

A good, fair critic is like a mirror. Try to dress, knot your tie, or comb your hair in a mirrorless room. Then examine the results. We all need mirrors.

The wisest of all kings said, "If you refuse criticism you will end in poverty and disgrace; if you accept criticism you are on the road to fame" (Prov. 13:18, Living Bible).

THE ART OF BEING CRITICIZED

Here are nine principles to use in accepting criticism:

(1) Be quiet while you are being criticized and make clear that you are listening.

(2) Look directly at the person talking to you.

(3) Under no condition find fault with the person who has just criticized you.

(4) Don't create the impression that the other person is destroying your spirit.

(5) Don't jest.

(6) Don't caricature the complaint.

(7) Don't change the subject.

(8) Don't imply that your critic has some ulterior, hostile motive.

(9) Convey to the other person that you understand his objection.

12. Taming the One-eyed Monster

*Type G1 Distortions: Uncritical Acceptance of
Media Messages as
Typified by Television*

The tall bent man wore a hearing aid and thick glasses, his
face a strange unexpressive mask from which looked out two
dull eyes. Obese and hunched from lack of exercise, he most
frequently responded to any statement: "You've got to be
kidding."

This poor specimen of stunted manhood may be showing
the effects of rock music on his ears, television on his body and
mind, and years of unscrupulous advertising upon his credu-
lity.

An exaggerated picture of our children in adulthood? Perhaps. But who knows? We've never raised a generation under
the circumstances that now exist. One researcher claimed that
the problem of trying to find the influence of modern media
upon children is that we have no children who have escaped
this exposure. So there is no standard against which to com-
pare this rising generation constantly bombarded with ear-
splitting music, mesmerized for years by a hypnotic video tube,
and so often conned by deceptive advertising.

The New Manipulators

Supposing you knew of a slick, fast-talking man, a first class
manipulator of people who, while keeping inside the law,
nevertheless made a good living by a series of questionable

deals in which he gave a lopsided picture of the goods he sold to unsuspecting customers. This voluble, lovable, half-rogue took a very keen interest in your ten-year-old-boy, and though you hoped he really appreciated your son for his own worth, you suspected he was setting you up, and aiming to get you through your son. Would you let your ten-year-old spend up to fifty-four hours per week with this character?

Well suppose no more. This is no fiction or phantasy but the grim reality of the advertising pitch aimed at children these days.

Commercial interests bring pressures to bear on your children that they would never dare to try upon their parents. The next time you are watching a TV program and you lament the inordinate number of commercials, just remind yourself that children's shows leave yours standing still. Your child is fed one commercial every four minutes of television viewing time, which is about twice the commercial diet of adult programs.

While at first you might be delighted with the news that your child's psychological make-up is constantly being examined by interested people, your delight may turn to despair when you realize the purpose that lies behind the process. As a result of all this research into the working of your son's psyche, all your offspring's psychological reactions, from latent sexuality, through sibling rivalry, to birth order anxiety, will be played upon in preparation for the moment of "untruth." This is when the vested interests, far more in earnest than any Pavlov conditioning his dogs, will zero in for the kill by pushing their products.

And to keep that youngster conditioned there is only one sure formula—repetition, repetition, repetition. In a rare moment of confession, one veteran of Madison Avenue admitted that at least three times, preferably five times, a week[1] he must expose the child to the mortar of titillation and manipulation concerning a particular product which cements the slight segments of program together.

When the advertising expert has sufficiently motivated your child, he will turn him on you and bring his not inconsiderable persuasive powers to bear on his parents. One television ad salesman claims that 70 percent of the kids ask their parents to buy products advertised on television and 89 percent of the parents do just what is requested.[2]

When you yield up your better judgment and buy the super-blastamatic-triple-powered-whamo, your guilt about spending so much money on such trivia may be assuaged by the realization that you have brought joy to your child's heart. But don't be so sure.

When the gadget fails to work after the first week, the disgusted child comes to feel that the whole advertising pitch is a gyp. In fact, he may begin to suspect much of what he is told. Possibly it is the start of the "credibility gap" that will lead him on the pathway of cynicism about the world of adults.

Video Boy

In the course of some experimental work, I spent an afternoon with a group of people at different levels of a hypnotic trance. The work proved to be fascinating, and as I left the office to drive home, I had a sense of gratitude for the opportunities of my work as a psychologist.

My poodle, Maximilian, met me at the door of my home and tail-wagged his way into my heart. As I proceeded through the den, I saw my son sitting with his eyes glued to the television screen. I greeted him with a casual hi, but there was no response. Just a trifle annoyed at his bad manners I retraced my steps.

I stopped and examined him carefully. He was in a hypnotic trance! Yes, there he was, the same immobile body, glazed eyes, complete lack of interest in anything but the matter of his concentration. Hypnotized by a video tube!

Of all the means of communication devised by the mind of man across the centuries, none has ever come within shouting distance of television. While the book and newspaper demand a man's eyes, allowing him to listen to what he will, and while radio calls for his ears and lets him use his eyes anyway he cares, this all-powerful communicator insists that he read and look, not just at still, monochrome images, but at a whole series of moving, compelling, and frequently colored figures reinforced by a subtle blanket of words and music. The house wife-viewer's senses may be so completely employed that only her sense of smell may recall her to the burning dinner in her oven.

James Baird the Englishman who coined the word *hypnosis* later came to regret his choice. Hypnosis from the Greek word *hypnos* suggested "sleep." Baird knew the hypnotized person was not asleep but in a shady, half-world between sleep and wakefulness. He preferred the term *monoideasism* as a better description of the phenomenon.

Hypnosis is the process whereby an individual concentrates on just one idea, eliminating everything else from his mind, and so comes under the sway of the suggester that he will almost unquestionably follow his behest.

Television monopolizes the viewer. It refuses to let him do anything but focus on its message, and the victim easily sinks into his comfortable, hazy, hypnotic trance, with all his will to do anything completely dissipated.

Children are the most susceptible subjects of all, and television takes advantage of them. Your child will spend more time with the TV set than he will with his parents, at his school, or in his church.

For better or for worse, television is undoubtedly the greatest single educational force in our society. The typical American high-school graduate will have spent some eleven thousand hours in classroom, but during this period of time he has been exposed to fifteen thousand hours of television.[3]

What does all this time spent in front of a television set do to your child?

Research has revealed:

Apparently it has little physical effect on him. There is no reliable evidence to show it will affect his eyes or posture.

He will spend thirty minutes a day less on play than did his pretelevision counterpart and will lose some valuable interpersonal experiences.

While well-validated studies do not show he spends less

time reading, I can personally vouch that my pre-TV child always read much more than his younger brother.

The age-old experience of a family gathered around the fire on a winter night, father reading to them, seems to have disappeared. Television has effectively replaced sessions of reading and storytelling.

"Video boy" is increasingly becoming a spectator of the events of life; and life at its best should be lived, not just observed.

Strangely enough his vocabulary may be extended, but will it be of much value for him to know all the ways of describing tobacco, beer, and toothpaste?

However, we have already noted the paucity of studies on the effects of television viewing on children, and we may have to draw some conclusions of our own. When we do this, most people discover just what they are looking for.

This is nowhere more clearly seen than in discussions concerning violence on TV and its effects on the viewer. In one city the TV stations in one week carried by count 7,887 acts of violence, and on Christmas night one Western program demonstrated the importance of peace on earth and goodwill toward man by showing 13 homicides.[4]

A research team, working with the National Commission on the Causes and Prevention of Violence, spent two weeks watching three network stations from 4:00 to 10:00 P.M. each day. When they had concluded, they added up 790 persons killed or injured during the programs which worked out to about 5 casualties for each program.[5]

Perhaps the most disquieting aspect of this study was that the typical persons committing the acts of violence were young married or middle-aged men. The victims were generally older people who fell before the attack of their younger adversaries.

It has been estimated that if your child is an average viewer in the years between five and thirteen, he may see as many as twelve thousand to thirteen thousand[6] human beings violently destroyed. What does this do to his idea of the importance of a human being of whom the Bible says the very hairs of his head are numbered?

The discussions of the effect of so much exposure to TV violence have reached three main conclusions:

(1) *The catharsis group*. This group argues that every individual has a certain residue of hostility within him, that it is natural for men to murder and destroy. If we provide programs of violence, it means the observers can vicariously live out their hostilities. This enables the viewer to get it out of his system.

It is strange that people will give credence to this theory when the catharsis concept is coming under fire from many psychotherapists. Some of these, including the writer, have seen people going through a catharsis experience and at the conclusion being more upset and hostile than they were at the beginning. The catharsis argument is of doubtful value.

(2) *The middle-of-the-road group*. Violence on television doesn't cause crime or aggression, but it can be a factor. According to this argument it is only when the child already has some type of emotional disturbance that his aggressiveness or hostility will be aroused by his TV viewing.

This argument has an element of sophistry in it. If the program arouses the impulses within the child, is it fair to say it "did not cause it"? Using more sedate language we may say that the video violence motivated him.

How does this fit in with the idea that I am my brother's keeper? What of the Pauline concept of concern for a weaker brother and what causes him to stumble?

(3) *The deeply concerned group*. This school of thought maintains that children constantly exposed to scenes of violence on TV and who spend so many hours in this violence world will come to feel that this is a normal way of life. In later days they may have little compunction about reproducing the activity they saw so vividly demonstrated on the screen to gain their own ends. For so long have they been fed the idea that force, deceit, fraud, manipulation, and seduction are the means of getting one's own way that they begin to develop a skepticism about the "square" world which calls for self-discipline, delay in satisfaction, and hard work as the pathway to success. The problem is obviously psychological.

While the process of personality development is complex,

one important component is identification. A child grows into adulthood by identifying with some adult. Once having decided on his model, he fashions himself after this individual.

In a home where there is no father and where the mother is away long hours seeking to make the living, TV becomes the babysitter. With whom will the imaginative child identify? The slippery glamorous thief or the dull muddle-headed Fred Flintstone? The options are many, but few of the models present the type of individual who will enable the child to become a good citizen through his identification.

A more unexpected aspect of television viewing may be the process of desensitization. A clinical psychologist placed a nine-year-old boy in a one-man theater and attached sensor wire to different parts of his body, measuring respiration, skin moisture, and heartbeat rate. He then ran a series of movies of the type frequently seen on TV. During the performance he carefully measured his subject's reactions.[7]

One of the most disturbing tentative conclusions was that TV may be creating what he calls "violence addicts." Constant exposure to violence causes a person to become completely insensitive to ferocity and force. Thus, we may be producing a generation of people who can unemotionally participate in acts of brutality.

Changing the Channels

The ancient Greeks told their children the story of Ulysses' voyages. On one occasion he and his men were captured by Polyphemus, a member of the Cyclops clan, and locked in a cave. It seemed as if there were no way of escape.

But the resourceful Ulysses had noticed that the members of the Cyclops group had only one eye and that was in the middle of their heads. Carefully Ulysses laid his plans. That night the Cyclops stretched himself across the entrance of the cave and soon drifted off to sleep. Ulysses and his men took a large piece of lumber and placed its end in the fire. When it was burning red hot, the leader and his crew lifted the burning beam to their shoulders and carried it over to the sleeping giant, held it aloft for a moment, then drove it down and put out his one eye.

So they made their escape.

TV is the one-eyed monster that captures your family, but you don't have to put out its eye—it's too expensive.

Any plan to use TV more effectively will have to proceed on a number of fronts:

Decide you're going to do something about the matter. Almost all authorities in the field agree that children's viewing habits should be limited. One study showed that less than 5 percent of families do anything about their children's time with TV.[8]

Limiting of TV viewing will have to be done in consideration of two factors—the amount of time spent with TV and the type of programs viewed.

One expert from the U.S. Office of Education has suggested one hour a day is ample time for a child's viewing. Others suggest perhaps one evening a week—perhaps Friday at the conclusion of school work.

Beware of using TV for reward and punishment. If the child is punished by not being allowed to view TV, he may come to think his parents value it so highly that they reward him by allowing him to watch.

Although the networks provide such sorry material for programs, they will quickly respond to criticism that parents are firmly responsible for what their children see. You must work out a "selective dialing" plan. One mother made a program guide for her children using pictures of a clock, a channel selector, and the TV program characters. Even the smallest children knew ahead of time just what programs were to be viewed at what time.

In making the selections try some co-viewing with your children. Point out to them the strong and weak points of programs; help them to come to a decision in which they feel they played a part.

Spend some time with them on the commercials. How is the sponsor trying to get you to buy his product? What factors should we have in mind when we are trying to decide what we will buy? What is the obvious shortcoming of the advertiser's pitch?

Never forget that only the family can provide some experiences vital for your child's development. Don't use TV as a means of keeping them "out of your hair." Let a moment of silence descend on your home and sit down and talk with the children.

Exercise your influence at the programming level. One of the glories of our democratic society is that everyone can play his part in influencing events of importance in our national life.

An ad man came up with the bright idea of the Frito Bandito, a happy, clean-shaven Mexican who by his quick-witted responses was able to con Anglos out of their Fritos. The idea caught on, and the ad was considered a great success. But many Mexicans objected to the commercial, and soon organizations protested what they called the racist message. The immediate response of the Frito Company was to promise that if the commercial offended a large group of people they would withdraw it.[9]

Be fair. When a good program is aired like the moon shots or the beginning of life, write to the networks and commend them. When objectionable material offends, write write, write. Mention the good program; then express your disappointment about the sorry program or commercial which they aired.

Make a triple approach. Write to the networks, the manager of the local station, and the sponsor. Remember the sponsor. He wants to sell his product, and if he feels he is antagonizing prospective customers, he will be willing to change things.

Recently someone lamenting the influence of TV said, "When it was mainly the movies, we could just insist that our children not go. Now that movie to which we objected is piped ino our house." While this is true, there is also an advantage in this situation. In our home we can view it *with* our children, and we can decide whether or not we'll have it displayed on the screen of our TV set.

All we really need is to want badly enough to do something about TV and we can do it. Type G Distortions manifest themselves in family members who have not sufficiently developed their critical faculties. If we don't, we will have a Cyclops that will educate, tyrannize, and finally completely control our homes.

—— OVER ⟶ TO ⟶ YOU ——

(1) As much as you might object to TV, you cannot ignore it. Check up on program offerings, help your children to select carefully, watch the programs along with the kids.

(2) Take a look at the offerings on noncommercial and public television. Some offerings here are the cream of the children's programming without the necessity of being subjected to some of hte les desirable types of commercials.

(3) Decide on a certain period when there will be no TV. Mealtimes, for example, should be kept free from the dominance of TV and provide opportunity for meaningful conversation.

(4) Many movies that are now appearing were made in a period when the movie industry despaired of family audiences who were in the house watching TV. Now the nonfamily movies are being beamed into your home. Keep an eye on these.

(5) In the 1975 season, action adventure programs ("a cherished network euphemism for shoot 'em ups," *Newsweek*) increased from 20 percent of prime time offering twenty years ago to 60 percent, and the networks introduced the idea of presenting material "suitable for family viewing" from 8:00 to 9:00 P.M. each evening. Express your gratitude for this development.

(6) However, don't be lulled into a false serenity. Remember the interpretation of "family viewing" may be rather flexible if not innocuous. Recollect too that one Neilson survey indicated that on one given evening five million kids under eleven years of age were glued to the tube between 10:00 and 11:00 P.M.

(7) Help your kids find some alternatives to TV—reading a book, games, visit to the park or museum.

13. You Heard, But Did You Listen?

Type G2 Distortions: Message Reaches the Brain but Is Not Comprehended

Mr. Henry is in a towering rage. Before he departed on his most recent business trip out of town, he'd given his son Ted a long lecture on the importance of watering his prize orchids. As he'd given the instructions, Mr. Henry was vaguely aware of Ted's casual attitude and easy countenance which said in effect, "Sure, pop, just leave it to me."

On his return Mr. Henry had hurried out to the greenhouse to find his precious plants in a wilted condition and giving evidence of Ted's neglect. So the older Henry proceeded to pour out his wrath on the head of his son who sat, with what he felt was commendable patience and tolerance, looking rather like some martyr being persecuted for his faith.

As Mr. Henry noticed this somewhat benign countenance of his son, something within him snapped, and at this moment, vividly aware of all his offspring's irresponsibilities and failures, he yelled, "Do you hear me?"

Of course, the boy heard him, all the household had heard him, even the neighbors across the street heard him. The problem was that Ted didn't *listen* to his father.

And this brings us to the importance of a person's listening if communication is to take place.

We have followed the journey of a message across six distortion points from the brain of one individual to the brain of another person in a process which, though it took the tiniest period of time, was nevertheless complex and involved. We might now imagine that the message reaching the brain would bring forth the described purpose of the speaker. Unfortunately, it now has to jump its greatest hurdle, for the receiver may not be listening.

Perhaps the problem is we didn't educate our children properly in the first place. Our educational processes have given little attention to teaching our children some of the all important verbal communication skills. Teaching the art of communication has focused primary attention upon the skills of reading and writing. With the growth of compulsory education in most countries in the nineteenth century, the main drive was to teach children the three r's with reading and writing as the major communication skills and a lesser emphasis on speaking. The fourth verbal skill of listening was virtually ignored.

All of this effort to make people literate was no real guarantee they could communicate proficiently. It had ignored the all-important oral aspects of communication.

Historically all human communication began as an oral process of speaking and listening. It continued on this level for centuries; then with the invention of the printing press the written word came to be considered a prime means of communication. With the invention and development of radio and television the stress has returned once more to oral communication.

As far as the family is concerned, oral communication is the major means by which people interact with one another. Few family members write essays to be read to the family. Some may write an occasional letter, but it will not be a particularly lengthy epistle as the parents discover when their children go off to college. Even the briefest of statements on a greeting card seem to represent a monumental effort in written communication between family members.

The Bible recognizes the primacy of oral communication in teaching the family. The classical passage concerning the teaching of children is found in the Book of Deuteronomy:

"Hear, O Israel: The Lord our God is one Lord:

"And thou shalt love the Lord thy God with all thine heart, and with all thy soul, and with all thy might.

"And these words, which I command thee this day, shall be in thine heart!

"And thou shalt teach them diligently unto thy children, and shalt talk of them when thou sittest in thine house, and when thou walkest by the way, and when thou liest down, and when thou risest up" (Deut. 6:4–7).

Note the way in which all the family activities are geared toward communicating the message of God to the children. The task is to be undertaken *diligently*, a word which means to "whet" or "sharpen," a sense captured in one version, "You shall whet and sharpen them so as to make them penetrate" (Deut. 6:7, Amplified Bible). The passage proceeds, ". . . and talk about them when you are at home or out for a walk; at bedtime and the first thing in the morning" (Deut. 6:7, Living Bible). Family life is characterized by a constant process of orally transmitting the message.

The great statement of faith in Deuteronomy is, "The Lord our God is one Lord: And thou shalt love the Lord thy God with all thine heart, and with all thy soul, and with all thy might," (Deut. 6:3 King James) but it is preceded by the call, "*Hear*, O Israel."

This note of the importance of listening is carried right through the Bible. In the New Testament our Lord urged his followers to listen some two hundred times over. Ever on his lips were statements such as, "He that hath ears to hear, let him hear," (Matthew 11:15 King James) and giving his gentle rebuke he asked his followers the question, "Having ears . . . hear ye not?" (Mark 8:18 King James).

In the light of this emphasis on listening it will be important that we teach our children to be listeners. As we noted earlier, parents must set the example so that imitative learning may take place. We begin by acquiring listening skills, no easy task, and then teach these skills to our children.

Work on Your Listening Inertia

Although many people may mention that the two words *hearing* and *listening* are synonyms, they are not. Actually they describe two different functions in the communication experience. *Hearing* describes the activity of a sound wave hitting your ear, and *listening* is the name we give to the process of sorting out the auditory stimuli.

The whole operation of a sound wave hitting the ear, and being transmitted to the brain, takes place with lightning speed. The brain itself is programmed by years of experience and conditioning to handle the auditory impressions with which it is fed. Like a busy executive's efficient secretary who sorts out the correspondence, keeping only the most important for his personal perusal, some sounds are summarily rejected, while others have the total attention focused on them.

This selective process carried on by the brain is the main distinction and difference between hearing and listening. From the total number of our auditory impressions we choose a small select number upon which to focus our attention. As the sounds come to us, we *hear*; when we apply ourselves to their meaning and significance, we *listen*.

As we discussed in an earlier chapter, we are living in a day when our environment is not only threatened by air pollution but also by *noise* pollution. Our ears are constantly bombarded by a multiplicity of sounds, and if we paid attention to all these sounds, it would drive us to distraction. So we develop— as a means of self-protection—an internal squelching mechanism by which we automatically reject certain sounds when they come to us. We develop a listening inertia.

Not unlike the ground crews of jet airlines who carefully position ear guards for protection against the ear-splitting sounds of the whining engines, modern man has had to develop a self-protective mechanism to defend himself from the constant acoustical bombardment of twentieth-century living. Most humans are engaged in a lifelong process of gradually building up their own personal internal ear plugs and training themselves to ignore certain sounds.

I once went to live in a house located near a railroad track. For the first few nights every passing train disturbed my sleep. As time went on, I grew to be less and less aware of the nearby activity. One evening a visitor inquired if the passing trains bothered me. I replied, "What trains?" My internal squelching mechanism had taken over so that I no longer listened to the railroad noises.

"You are an airline pilot flying a four-engine jet from New York to Los Angeles. There are 72 people aboard, including 9 children, 18 married couples, 22 businessmen, and 5 crew members. The plane leaves New York at 5:10 P.M. and arrives in Los Angeles 6 hours and 32 minutes later. What was the pilot's name?"

The first four words give you the answer. However, most people miss it because (1) it is a little bit tricky, and (2) listening is an active task. Most of us are not willing to work at it.

There is obviously wisdom in the natural tendency we have *not to listen.* The mechanism protects us in many ways, but it also does us a disservice. It causes us to miss many of the things to which we should listen. A really observant person has to work hard to overcome what we might call "listening inertia."

All of this means work—hard work—if we are going to get the message that comes to our ears.

Leftover Time

One of the problems with listening is that we have time to spare. While some speakers may verbalize at about 125 words a minute, most of us can think about four times that speed. As the speaker presents his ideas, we can easily move along and keep up with him. It is so simple that we have time on our hands, so we can occasionally dart ahead or go on a side excursion. These side excursions are particularly damaging and lead to our downfall as listeners.

As you sit in an audience listening to a speaker, you may move along with him for a short period. Then a picture of the office flashes onto the screen of your mind, and you see the work awaiting your attention. So you take a mental trip back to your place of toil, look over your correspondence, check up on your coffee-drinking secretary, and then rejoin the speaker.

A little later in the discourse the golf course begins to

beckon, and off you go. You bask in the warm sun, admire the condition of the greens, see the old cronies. Mentally you visualize the beautiful drive, the flawless putt, your opponent's dismay, and the concluding moment of triumph.

But on one of these side journeys you stay away too long, and when you return, it is to discover that the speaker has gotten so far ahead that there is no chance of catching him. So you sink into a passive resignation to your horrible fate, put a fixed look on your face, and hope the speaker will soon tire and quit.

The good listener doesn't go on side excursions. He tries to anticipate where the speaker is going—gets out ahead like a scout on wagon train. As soon as he realizes the speaker is going in another direction, he hurries back and rejoins him.

Capturing the Balloons

The process of a speaker addressing an audience has been envisaged in a number of different ways. One older method was to imagine that each listener had a funnel-like appurtenance fitting on the top of his head. The speaker carried his store of ideas like water in a bucket and conceived his chief task as pouring ideas into the funnel-heads of his auditors.

Because of his distance from the funnel-heads, the speaker was forced to resort to tossing out his buckets of ideas, hoping his aim would be good enough to slosh at least some tiny droplets into the funnels. Thus, the listener was a passive recipient, and the number of ideas he received depended mainly on the throwing ability of the speaker.

A much more productive way for the lecturer to see his audience would be to change them from funnel-heads to something more like women sitting in the beauty shop with roller-covered heads. These roller-like contraptions are bumps of knowledge complete with tie-on strings. They are the concepts already possessed by the listeners, and the protruding strings are waiting for familiar thoughts and concepts to be attached.

The communicator on the platform is launching balloons inscribed with messages printed in large letters. Each of his idea-balloons trails a long string, making it a simple matter for the listener to grasp it as it passes by.

While much of the speaker's ability lies in his capacity to adapt his idea-balloons so that they match the more obvious tie-down spots on his auditors' heads, the listener is no quiescent squeezed-out sponge. The listener's activity is just as important in communication as the speaker's skill.

A prospective listener sits in an audience. The speaker launches his balloons and sends them floating across the room trailing their strings. As they sail toward the listener, he is faced with the responsibility for some action and has at least three alternatives.

He may be bodily present but only partly conscious. In his sleepy mistiness he is only vaguely aware of his surroundings. The idea-balloons drift lazily by. For all he knows they may only be spots before his eyes; so he pays them scant attention, content to relax in the twilight zone of inattentive half-sleep.

Or perhaps the balloons look a little unusual, and for a brief moment he toys with the possibility of closer acquaintance. But they are a trifle strange and bear little relationship to the bumps on his head. After a casual glance he lets them drift on their way.

A third possibility is that the listener may examine the balloons very closely. He notes even the slightest resemblances to the stringed bumps on his head. As the balloons come closer he becomes more intent. He is enthralled with the potential of these concepts. He searches his mind for associated ideas. He reaches out, takes a firm grip on the strings, and begins to tie them securely to his previous knowledge. These new ideas are now his. This third attitude is a must for the listener.

The High Art of Concentration

One of the popular stories of hospital life tells of two doctors meeting in the hospital corridor. The orthopedic surgeon is commiserating with the psychiatrist, "I don't know how you can spend all your day listening to people . . ."

The psychiatrist replies, "Who listens?"

Who indeed? Listening is really hard work. It calls for the expenditure of effort in concentrating to defeat our listening inertia. Listening cannot be carried on as a part-time activity; it must be entered into with all the vigor we can muster.

Returning from the rural area where I was pastoring my first church, I thrilled with excitement at the prospect of seeing my former pastor. I had so many stories to tell him. Entering his office, we shook hands and then sat down as I started to recount my story.

Bubbling over with enthusiasm, I poured out my tale. To my amazement my friend didn't even look me in the eyes. He straightened up his desk top, pushed sundry pens and pencils into place, leaned over to pull out a drawer, and moved around its contents. Now and then he half-glanced my way.

My story slowed down. Its importance gradually diminished, and finally I limped to a conclusion, made a lame excuse, and left his office. It was one of the most disappointing encounters of my life.

In a later frank interview the man told me he had really been interested in what I had to tell but just wanted to make the most use of his time, hence his tidying-up effort. He might have finished with a neat desk, but he had ruined a relationship. He had not learned to listen.

During World War II, Australian women industriously knitted socks for soldiers. At any and every meeting they considered it their patriotic duty to keep the knitting needles constantly on the move. They undoubtedly were the most difficult of all groups to which to speak. Clicking needles and vacant faces that told the story of mental calculations of stitches and patterns were absolutely no inspiration for a speaker.

And make no mistake about it: A listening audience is more than half the secret of any successful speech. A group with any sizable number of people who refuse to take an interest in the speaker can transform an eloquent orator into a halting, hesitant, dry-as-dust talker.

Since writing the foregoing I stumbled upon a passage from the writings of Charles Haddon Spurgeon. Sometimes called the "Prince of Preachers," Spurgeon was one of the adornments of the Victorian era. Five or six thousand people jammed his church, morning and evening, every Sunday for years. With no musical instruments or complex educational organization in his church, the sermon was the main feature of the service. This brilliant orator had a preaching ability rarely heard before or since.

Among other activities he organized a theological college for the training of ministers. His lectures to these students are gems of wit and wisdom. In one of the lectures on the subject of "attention" he voiced his reaction to inattentive auditors: ". . . . they are not in the habit of attending. They attend the chapel but do not attend to the preacher. They are accustomed to look around at every one who enters the place, and they come in at all times, sometimes with much stamping, squeaking of boots, and banging of doors. I was preaching once to a people who continually looked around, and I adopted the expedient of saying, 'Now, friends, as it is so very interesting to you to know who comes in, and it disturbs me so very much for you to look around, I will, if you like, describe each one as he comes in, so that you may sit and look at me, and keep up at least a show of decency.' I described one gentleman who came in, who happened to be a friend whom I could depict without offense, as 'a very respectable gentleman who had just taken his hat off,' and so on; and after that one attempt I found it was not necessary to describe any more, because they felt shocked at what I was doing, and I assured them that I was much more shocked that they should render it necessary for me to reduce their conduct to such absurdity. It cured them for the time being, and I hope for ever, much to their pastor's joy."[1]

The distressed preacher went on to describe how people who were not listening affected him. He maintained that he wanted all eyes fixed on him and all ears opened to him. He added, "To me it is an annoyance if even a blind man does not look me in the face."[2]

What was true of the preacher and his audience is equally true of the speaker and his listener. The way in which the listener pays attention to a conversational partner will in a large measure determine the quality of the conversation.

Although nonprofessionals refer to a deaf person's *lipreading*, some professionals are not enthusiastic about the use of this term. They point out that the so-called lipreader doesn't just look at the lips but receives a number of visual cues. Some of them prefer the term *visual listening*. The same principle applies to people who may have the acutest hearing: If you are to get the message, you must not listen with your ears alone but also visually read by concentrating on the speaker.

If you are going to be an effective listener, you must give the speaker your undivided attention. It is his moment, and every aspect of your demeanor must say, "Come on. Let's have it. You're in the center of the stage in my thinking."

The good listener doesn't do a lot of things. He cannot lean back in his chair with eyes half-closed as if he were taking his afternoon nap—none of those furtive looks as if mentally cataloging the books on his shelves. He doesn't steal glances at his watch with the inference, "Time is up; you've been here long enough." He won't doodle on a pad as though preparing an entry for a museum of modern art.

The good listener is relaxed. The telephone is cared for, his secretary warned against interruptions. He leans slightly toward the speaker, his eyes focused on him, not in a staring match, but in a coaxing, interested manner. Every aspect of the listening one says, "Tell me more."

Watch your speaker blossom as he becomes aware of the situation. See the way in which he drops his defenses; note the growing confidence in his bearing. Far too long he has been on the receiving end, and now he has a chance to express his ideas.

The good listener is a man with a mission. Every power of body and mind is focused on the listening task.

OVER ⟶ TO ⟶ YOU

Try an exercise in listening. Listen to someone talking—a political or an after-dinner speaker, a preacher, or a troubled person who wants to tell his story. Enter actively into the experience in the following ways:

* Start with a determination to overcome your listening inertia. Like the naval message, give yourself a strong and certain "Now hear this."

* Examine the facts as they are presented, and try to determine if they are accurate or are just being presented to prove a point or used to bolster a case.

* Look for a message beyond the words. The changing tones and fluctuating facial expressions, gestures, and bodily movements all carry a message.

* The speaker may have something to say that you need to hear. Decide not to let your prejudice block you from appreciating and evaluating the message.

* Fight distractions. Refuse to be lured away by your curiosity. Reject the incidentals, interruptions, and any peripheral activity.

* Try to anticipate where the speaker is going. Scout on ahead. If he goes on another trail, retrace your steps and rejoin him.

* Focus your attention on the theme or main message. See how other material bolsters this basic idea.

* Make mental summaries periodically so that you know where you've been and have a launching pad for what follows.

* Underline the illustrations and examples. They will become easily remembered reference points.

14. The Other Dimension

Although medieval cathedrals are today seen as architectural masterpieces, they were first and foremost instruments of communication, and not primarily from the pulpit to the listener standing first on one leg and then the other, or seated on crude, uncomfortable benches. In the spirit of a people emerging from the Dark Ages, during which church buildings had been broad, squat blobs on the landscape, the children of the Renaissance built their cathedrals with spires pointing like giant fingers to pierce the sky. These fingers led the beholders' eyes upward to an omnipotent God whose ways and thoughts were far above anything mortal man could do or think.

To support the towering walls, flying buttresses were added, tapestries of stone which, though functional, enhanced and beautified the soaring walls and towers. Even the mundane drain pipes channeling off the rain from the roof became gargoyles, strange peculiar faces, personifying the very real demon world of which the clergy spoke, spitting out the waste water through their pursed lips.

Sitting or standing inside the building, the peasant gazed in awe at the vaulted ceilings and elaborately carved woodwork telling the message of a God of infinite glory and majesty. Like diamonds in gigantic stone settings the elaborately fashioned stained-glass windows cast their dim religious light. Those windows communicated the clearest message of all. In a sequence around the church, they told the story of God and man, from the beginning of creation through the history of Israel, the life and death of Jesus Christ, and on to the vivid portrayal of the holocaust at the end of all things. Never having been able to read the manuscripts so carefully hoarded in the scriptorium for the educated clergy to read and copy, the peasant gazed in awe at the gigantic cartoon of the windows and wandered from window to window following the visualized story of God's dealing with man. Stained-glass windows weren't just beautiful works of art done for the glory of God; they were the visualized story set forth for the religious education of man.

I wandered into a beautiful, recently finished church building, a modern version of the ancient gothic, replete with the beautiful stained-glass windows. But irony of ironies: In this building preserving the heritage of the medieval cathedral, the windows were modernized, done in contemporary patterns, jumbled and juxtaposed hues of many colors. To discover what the window represented it was necessary to have a guide who struggled to explain the symbolism.

What in ancient times had been the means of telling of God's dealing with man has become a confused decorative piece to which people look with uncomprehending eyes and murmur, "Beautiful," "Lovely hues," and receive no message from God or man. The windows, once a means of instruction, have become a mere ornamentation, a status symbol—"Our church has such pretty stained-glass windows." But they communicate no other message.

Many modern families are like these church windows. Across the centuries the family has been the closely knit intercommunicating unit, the primary source of information, education, and support. With the advent of modern times and in an increasingly impersonal world where the family should be in Tofler's words, "the shock absorber of society," communication has become increasingly distorted, and duologue rather than dialogue has characterized the family's communication.

Duologue is a new word which describes a type of conversation allegedly carried on by two or more people. In actual fact, a duologue is a monologue which one person carries on before a disinterested audience or with another individual. Some observers feel they have a beautiful example of a duologue in the classroom where the professor talks and the students don't listen; then the students talk and the professor gives up paying attention.

About the only thing that distinguishes a duologue from a monologue is that the participants take it in turns. You ramble on in your talking until some other member of the group gives the signal he wants a turn by clearing his throat or mumbling or gazing vacantly around the room. You keep on as long as you decently can; then you reluctantly let him have the floor.

Even as you give him his opportunity, you ready yourself. Now and then you pay him the compliment of laughing at a passingly funny remark; then you proceed to emit your signals by looking absent-mindedly out of the window, lapsing into silence, or making vague "uhs." Once he slows or hesitates, you jump in.

A good illustration of a duologue would be a man sitting before a TV. There is no real interchange, no emotion, no intimacy. He and the set have nothing in common. They endure each other. The viewer has the edge in this situation since he can switch off the set when he tires of it.

The best example of a duologue, of course, would be a number of television sets tuned in to different channels and facing each other. Each spews out its unending stream, paying no attention to any of the others, and the only hope is that one or all of them will blow a picture tube.

Family members are probably the most skillful practitioners of the duologue. One wife was asked, "Do you and your husband talk to each other?" She responded, "Oh, yes, we talk to each other. The only problem is listening to each other." Tragically, the main lesson they have learned in their years of living together and interacting with each other is to be completely indifferent.

The family might be likened to a number of porcupines huddled together on an icy night. They need each other's warmth to insure at least a modicum of comfort. However, their very closeness brings its own problems and raises the possibility they may stick each other. They have to learn the secret of living in such close proximity, giving and receiving warmth without each damaging the other.

They undoubtedly have a potential for hurting as well as helping. One alarming piece of research quoted the old bit of doggerel:

> Lizzie Borden took an ax
> And gave her father forty whacks
> When the job was neatly done
> She gave her mother forty-one.

The writer then proceeds to produce some alarming statistics about family conflicts and goes as far as to refer to "the family as a cradle of violence" and show that family fights constitute the largest category of police calls. He further claims, "Family members physically abuse each other far more often than do nonrelated individuals."[1] All of this occurs within the institution ordained of God for the reproduction and nurture of the race. These family members obviously have to learn the art of living together and deriving all the benefits of the warmth and relationship within their group without damaging each other.

The arid plains of West Texas present some unusual surprises, such as the news that shrimp are now being nurtured and harvested in the highly saline artificial lakes whose locales are as far removed from the seaside as could be imagined. That desert land literally "blossoms as the rose" when subterranean water is supplied. As water is pumped up and channeled across the land, it produces an abundant harvest.

In this type of operation it all depends on the channels. If the channels are kept open and if the life-giving water is allowed to flow, the land will produce amazing crops. But if those channels are blocked and the flow hindered, the soil will deteriorate into arid desert. Family relationships are like this.

If dialogue is "that address and response between persons in which there is a flow of meaning between them in spite of all the obstacles that normally would block the relationship," we should work at clearing away all the obstacles.

There are some special resources that must be utilized in this task of strengthening family life. For years I have tried to communicate mainly through writing and speaking, occasionally by means of the electronic media, but I now feel the most dramatic single moment in my communicating career came through an effort as an amatuer printer on a crude printing press. Visiting the Gutenberg Museum in Mainz, Germany, we stood looking at the historic Gutenberg Bible, the first book ever printed with movable type. Johann Gutenberg invented the movable type-printing technique in Mainz in the fifteenth century. We gazed with awe at the historic treasure.

From the room housing this historic volume we moved down a stairway to view the reconstructed workroom of the pioneer printer. I marveled that such heavy wooden machinery could have been invented and built in the fifteenth century and was absorbed in the work of the demonstrator-printer as he made preparation for printing a page on the historic machine. Apparently becoming aware of my intense interest, the demonstrator turned and invited me to try my hand at printing.

Following his direction and supervision, I inserted the paper, lowered the frame to hold it in place, pushed the type bed into position in the press, then took hold of the six-foot-long lever that screwed down the pressure. Taking a firm grip, I pulled it across in much the same manner as Johann Gutenberg had five hundred years previously and printed the page. Moving the lever back to its original position, we pulled out the bed of the press to remove the parchment paper.

As I stood and gazed in awe, I realized that in my hand was a page I had printed—a portion of the living Word of God that had been so influential in changing the world of that day.

I prize that manuscript page and have had it framed and hung in a special spot on the wall of my office. Whenever a guest comes in, I make sure he sees the treasured parchment. One day af riend made a difficult request, "Please read it to me."

I responded, "I'm sorry, it's in Latin; I cannot read it."

Too often our Bibles are like that historic manuscript page of mine—ornate, decorative, revered, but not read or put into practice. The tragedy of this is that the Bible has much to say to us.

Probably the most dramatic communications systems are those associated with satellites stationed in outer space, reflecting messages back to distant spots on the earth. From the first communication satellite *Courier*, a whole group—Telstars, Relays, Early Birds—operated on the basis of small vehicles, conveying relatively weak transmitters, sending signals to receivers connecting into sophisticated, highly developed national communications systems. Poor and technically backward nations without sophisticated communications networks were at a disadvantage.

All of this changed on the morning of May 30, 1974, when a satellite named *ATS-6* roared off from Cape Kennedy and went into a synchronous orbit that kept it stationary, hanging in space 22,300 miles over the Galapagos Islands. *ATS-6* is equipped with a special thirty-foot antenna for collecting relatively weak transmissions and beaming them to small stations on the earth.

This has become the world's first direct satellite. The entirely new approach means that instead of signals being fed into national communications systems where they could be routed to their destinations, messages are pulled directly into the homes of individuals.

All of this may have a lesson for us. Far too long we've been hoping for a new way of life—laws, programs, agencies—but in vain. Perhaps the time has finally come for us to take the message into individual homes, a message Almighty God has been beaming toward men and women across the eons of time.

Epilogue

Slowly, apprehensively, the man walked to the foot of the looming hill. The sky above was an enormous blue-black velvet drape, and away from the competing lights of the town the stars sparkled in a vivid whiteness against the backdrop of night.

As he walked, strange thoughts chased themselves through his mind. He'd come out here to get away from his fellow humans, but the image of one—his mother—came clearly into focus. He couldn't understand it at the time, but he vividly remembered the night they'd talked together. A casual discussion slipped into a moment of deep confidentiality as she told him about the book-burning episode.

The new, so-called people's government, from which they'd hoped so much, had developed a peculiar paranoia. They were anxious to be rid of all dangerous ideas and so handed down lists of prescribed books that were to be destroyed. Among these were the books of religion, the opiate of the masses; every vestige of this superstition must be stamped out.

Then a strange note in his mother's voice, "Worst of all they burned the Bibles . . . every single Bible." Tears flooded her pale blue eyes and a look of horror spread over her wrinkled face, "God forgive them—not a single Bible left in the town."

He wandered along the vaguely delineated trail. In school he often heard mention of this strange collection of myths and fables. Why had they needed to destroy the Bible?

Some strange thoughts had been bothering him recently: "What about this superstitious God idea?"

A maelstrom of emotions engulfed him. Then he stopped, looked up into the black-starred canopy, and cupped his hands to his mouth. With an intensity that aroused a strange awe within himself, he shouted, "God, are you there?"

And the God with whom man needs so desperately to communicate is not afar off and hiding. He is, as the poet put it, the "Hound of Heaven," searching for his erring creatures.

God is forever seeking man. The fundamental question to a disobedient Adam was, "Where art thou?" The history of man has been of a God seeking to communicate with his rebellious children.

In the rough and turbulent days in ancient Israel known as the period of the judges, the Bible tells us, "Messages from the Lord were very rare in those days." (I Sam 3:1 Living Bible) The implication is that in the struggle for power and material possessions the people ceased to listen to the God who sought to communicate with them.

The mysterious call came to the boy Samuel at work in the temple, and the priest Eli gave him instructions as to the way he should respond. Lying on his simple cot, the boy heard the call and responded, "Yes, I am listening" (I Sam 3:10 Living Bible).

"I am listening." God needs men and women who will adopt the same attitude as the boy Samuel and hear a sure word for these troubled times.

Significantly, the figure used to describe Jesus in John's gospel is "the Word." Jesus Christ was God's word to men and women, and as he hung on the cross, he reached one hand up to a holy God and one down to sinful man and sought to bring us back together again.

Living in this megaphonic era, pounded by the cacophony of a jillion voices, we need above everything else to hear the word of our Lord Jesus Christ who came to establish our communication with God.

There is no need to cry up at the sky. All we need is just an awareness of failure, a willingness to ask forgiveness through faith in Christ. Then the most miraculous of all communication takes place—"Thy sins are forgiven thee"—and frail human beings become the sons and daughters of the living God.

Notes

Introduction

1. William V. Haney, *Communication and Organizational Behavior* (Homewood, Ill.: Irwin D. Dorsey, 1973), pp. 181–82.

Chapter 1

1. Helen Keller, *Teacher: Ann Sullivan Macy* (Garden City, NY: Doubleday, 1955), p. 8.
2. *World Book Encyclopedia* (Chicago: Field Enterprizes Educational Corporation, 1964), 2:209.
3. Helen Keller, *The Story of My Life* (New York: Doubleday, Doran, and Co., 1933), p. 23.
4. Ibid., p. 25.

Chapter 3

1. See Judg. 12:6.
2. John W. Drakeford, *Farewell to the Lonely Crowd* (Waco, Tex.: Word Books, 1969), p. 89.
3. Preserved Smith, *The Life and Letters of Martin Luther* (Boston: Houghton Mifflin, 1911), p. 179–180.

Chapter 4

1. Fred Belliview and Lin Richter, *Understanding Human Sexual Inadequacy* (Boston: Little, Brown, and Co., 1970), p. 219.
2. Gerald I. Nierenberg and Henry H. Calero, *How to Read a Person Like a Book* (New York: Hawthorne Books, Inc.).

Chapter 5

1. Haney, *Communication and Organizational Behavior*, p. 362.

Chapter 8

1. Nardi Reeder Campion, "Ask Don't Tell," *Reader's Digest* (August, 1966), p. 51.

2. Frank Capra, *The Name Above the Title* (New York: Macmillan, 1971), p. 346.

Chapter 11
1. Whittaker Chambers, *Witness* (New York: Random House, 1952), p. 16.

Chapter 12
1. "The Audience," *Time*, 26 January 1968, p. 55.
2. "The TV Generation," *Changing Times* (July, 1968), p. 46.
3. Ibid.
4. "Is TV Brutalizing Your Child?" *Look*, 2 December 1969.
5. *Research Roundup*, Research and Statistics Department, Sunday School Board of the Southern Baptist Convention, 29 August 1969.
6. "How Dangerous Is TV Violence?" *Parents* (October, 1969), p. 60.
7. "Tracks that Violence Leave," *Life*, 30 January 1970, p. 57.
8. "Should Children's TV Habits Be Controlled?" *Good Housekeeping* (March, 1968), p. 193.
9. *Newsweek*, 22 December 1969, p. 86.

Chapter 13
1. Helmut Thielicke, *Encounter with Spurgeon* (Philadelphia: Fortress Press, 1963), p. 236–37.
2. Ibid., p. 235.

Chapter 14
1. Suzanne K. Steinnetz and Murray A. Straus, "The Family As Cradle of Violence," *Readings in Marriage and Family 75/76* (Guilford, Conn.: Dushkin Group, Inc.), p. 113.